The Black Ghost of Scotia & More Pennsylvania Fireside Tales

(Origins and Foundations of Pennsylvania Mountain Folktales and Legends - Vol. II)

By Jeffrey R. Frazier

My heart's in the highlands ,
*   my heart is not here*
My heart's in the highlands,
*   a'chasin' the deer*
A'chasin' the wild deer,
*   and followin' the roe*
My hearts in the highlands,
*   wherever I go*

                    Robert Burns

The Black Ghost of Scotia and More Pennsylvania Fireside Tales

By Jeffrey R. Frazier

Cover :
The monument on Indian Lane
Potter Township, Centre County
(See Story number XI in this volume)

Previous page:
Wolf howling at the misty moon; drawn by James J. Frazier

To my children, James & Kay,
who, I hope, will always carry a
piece of my Pennsylvania mountains
somewhere in their hearts.

Table of Contents

List of Photos

INTRODUCTION

In offering a second volume of Pennsylvania mountain legends and folktales to the reading public, the author does so with a note of appreciation to all who found the first volume of legends of interest - public and press alike. The old stories and folktales which appeared in my *Pennsylvania Fireside Tales* and which seemed to strike a "chord" within me, also apparently appealed to others as well. Most people like these survivors from a bygone day - a time that was simpler in many ways than this present hectic age.

People also seem to agree with me that the Pennsylvania mountains and streams that were the "stage" for these human interest tales are as worthy of preservation as the stories themselves - a point that I indirectly tried to impress upon readers of the first volume, and which, in recent years, has often become a secondary consideration to those who would rather quarry, pave, or develop the state's natural beauty away. This attitude, however, is not entirely a new one.

It has been said that the story of the Pennsylvania frontier is one of the ax, the plow, and the rifle. When the first white men came to what is now Pennsylvania, they were overwhelmed with the "endless" forests that had to be cleared in order to find space for homes and fields. Using their plows and axes, it took settlers long hours of unremitting toil to make the land a tolerable place to live. But even after these pioneers had tamed some of the forest and had built their homesteads, there were always reminders of the wilderness that surrounded them.

There was, of course, the dense forest that seemed to stretch on forever, as well as a profusion of insects and insect sounds, the like of which they had never encountered in Europe. Then, too, there were the nightly sounds of wolves, panthers, bobcats, and other wild animals that could send chills up the spines of the faint-hearted. But some people seemed to thrive on the isolation, particularly those hardy frontiersmen known as the Scotch-Irish.

Descendants of Englishmen and Scotchmen who flocked to Ireland in the early part of the seventeenth century to occupy rebel lands confiscated by King James the First, these "Ulstermen", as they were called in England, migrated to Pennsylvania about seventy-five years later. Known for his independent spirit, it was sometimes said that a Scotch-Irishman could make a home in the wilderness if he were just given some good whisky, a sharp ax, and the Holy Bible. There were some practical reasons for this desire for solitude, and one was that the more isolated a family was, the less competition they had for the game they needed to kill for food. It was partly because of its utility as a hunting tool that the rifle figures prominently in the story of the Pennsylvania frontier, but its role as an instrument of war is a major part of the story as well.

Competition for land and for hunting rights not only arose among white settlers in Pennsylvania, but also led to conflicts with native Americans. The white man's appetite for land seemed to be insatiable, and the Indians kept moving west to escape the scourge. Whenever the Indians would see rats, which had never been seen before in America until they were imported on the white man's ships, or would see honey bees, also a white man's phenomenon, they began to learn that settlers were not far behind and would soon be moving in to claim more land for themselves. It was this continuous grasping that finally led to the "border wars" of Pennsylvania, and which created another entire body of folktales and legends, some of which are included in this volume. Consequently, not only did the early settlers here have to contend with all the rigors of the wilderness in order to survive, but also had fo fight those who were really the rightful owners of the land.

So what some of the stories in this volume convey, then, are the ordeals the first settlers had to endure in conquering the wilderness that was once Pennsylvania. In fact, after reading about some of these ordeals, the reader may quickly, and correctly, come to the conclusion that the mountains produced men and women of a different type. Indeed it was the mountains of Pennsylvania that nurtured men like Daniel Boone, born near Birdsboro, Berks County, and many of the best officers of the Revolutionary War, who were "trained" while taking part in the border wars that were fought upon these dark and rugged hills.

Lest we forget, however, despite the seemingly impossible hardships they had to endure, these early Pennsylvanians were not superhuman. Their minds worked in the same way ours do, and, just like the rest of us, they had the same basic needs, desires, and fears. They did, after all, eat and drink many of the same things we do, and they laughed and cried about situations that make us laugh and cry. They also wore dresses, shirts, and pants that were much like ours; and when it came to putting those pants on, they didn't jump into them in some superhuman way. On the contrary, just like you and I, they put them on in the normal way: one leg at a time.

On the other hand, the men and women that struggled through and triumphed over the demands of pioneer life had to be people of a tougher breed. They had to endure and move on, and from them came the sturdy stock of people that had the persistence to conquer the wilderness that was Pennsylvania. Consequently, it is no wonder that love of and devotion to our mountains seems to be ingrained in the descendants of the old pioneers: the hunters who scour the woods each spring and fall, the fisherman who sit along sparkling waters that bubble forth from cool mountain springs, and the hikers who tread upon the same ground that may have once echoed with the sounds of Indians' footsteps.

To some Pennsylvanians, the state's mountain trails become as familiar as city streets are to the city dweller. For example, it used to be said of Joe Varner, an old-time lumberman in Juniata County, that if he were blindly dropped off in any spot in the mountains within ten miles of his hometown of Arch Rock, he would know where he was and could find his way back home. Joe Varner might be surprised to find that, even today, many of those remote spots haven't changed too much at all.

It is to the credit of Pennsylvania's many outdoorsmen that forest conditions and game populations in numerous parts of the state have been preserved as well as they have. Hunters fought for the reclamation of the lands left scarred by strip miners, and hikers and hunters alike fought equally hard to renew and regulate the forest lands left devastated by lumber kings or coveted by power companies. It is through the efforts of many such far-sighted individuals that there exist the state forests and natural areas that we have today - forests that contain some of the finest hunting country in the United States. As an added bonus, it is probably the presence of wild and scenic country like this that helped many of the old ways and old stories to linger on as long as they have. In turn, these "survivors" not only help to perpetuate that feeling of kinship some of us feel toward these rugged Pennsylvania hills, but also connect us to a rich fabric of history and to the people who lived it.

More Pennsylvania Fireside Tales

These are the tales the reader will find in this book - folktales and legends that seem to capture and hold the imagination; stories whose roots can be found in the first half of the twentieth century, or even stretching back to the time of the Civil War and beyond. But what is it, exactly, that makes such stories intriguing? Perhaps legends and folktales are collected, preserved, and retold for some of the same reasons that antiques are collected and carefully maintained. Certainly one reason people seek out antiques is because these scarce items are a good financial investment. But there are also other reasons that relics of the past are sought and preserved.

For one thing, they are a link or connection with previous generations. They cause us to feel closer to the past; our life's span seems extended, and we seem less mortal. Legends and folktales do the same thing. However, with antiques we can see, feel, and use tangible items that have actually been handled by real people in years gone by. With folktales and legends, on the other hand, we are dealing with intangibles.

To be appreciated, the tales should be thought of as true stories, but they often stretch our credibility. Their very content, many times so fantastic and unbelievable, often precludes any belief in factual origins. Nonetheless, if the exaggerations and the embellishments are removed, there are a few core sentences left that might be worth reevaluating. It is in this distillate of one or two core sentences that we can find any kernels of truth that may exist. However, in many cases the sentences left to ponder would still relate a tale so fantastic-sounding that most people would dismiss further study as nothing more than a useless exercise.

After all, in these modern days with television, VCR's, personal computers, and all the other conveniences we have at our fingertips, it seems difficult to think that tales of ghosts, witches, wolves, panthers, wild Indians, or larger-than-life heroes, are anything more than products of vivid imaginations; nothing other than fanciful stories concocted in the minds of gifted story tellers. Nonetheless, there have always been those who have liked to think that many of the old legends and folktales are grounded in truth, even if just in indirect ways. In other words, each tale can be seen as its own little mystery, and it was with this idea that I began to collect and analyze Pennsylvania's own mountain stories.

At the very least, I reasoned, there would be the sheer enjoyment of getting back into the woods once in a while. I would be able to visit favorite spots and relive, somewhat, the Tom Sawyer type boyhood that I experienced growing up in the mountains. My expectations were more than met, and, much to my delight, I found that tellers of the old tales could still be found. As an added bonus, I found that these folks were always more than willing to talk about the old days and entertain the avid listener with stories that had been passed down the generations. Without exception, the "old-timers" I spoke with, and even the not-so-old who had heard the tales from parents or grand parents, were usually able to impart a story or a memory worth recording. In fact, one of the things that I have learned from the many years of collecting tales in out-of-the-way spots was that every valley, mountain, stream, and old house here in the Keystone State probably has a unique and compelling story about it if the right person had been asked.

Certainly many of the folks who related their stories to me were often unique in that they had grown up in a rural way of life that will never be seen again. They were born and raised in an age we now call "The Good Old Days" - a period now remembered as a slower-paced, less-materialistic, era when family ties were unbroken by distance and time. It was an epoch when farms did not yet have electricity, and cars, television, and most modern labor-saving devices were things of the future. Necessarily, these "Good" Old Days were ones of scarcity and making do with what one had. "Everyone was poor", was the way one person put it to me, but one thing that did seem plentiful in those times, compared to today, was legends and folktales.

The old tales most certainly were abundant at one time, given the number that were still around when I started collecting back in 1970. Moreover, not only were the stories I hoped to collect still here, but they were, in many cases, legends whose roots, I was later to determine, went back far beyond the Civil and Revolutionary Wars. For instance, the Germanic and Celtic origins of some of the stories I collected became obvious upon reading books like *Grimm's Fairy Tales*, J. F. Campbell's *Popular Tales of the West Highlands*, John Fiske's *Myths and Mythmakers*, and many other similar works.

Despite these often-ancient roots, it seemed that it was never a problem finding someone who could tell me another old-time story or legend. However, many readers will, no doubt, say "It's too bad he couldn't have gotten grandpa's (or grandma's) stories", and yes, it is too bad, for there were undoubtedly many others whose tales would have added much to the treasures I had already found. Nonetheless, a point was reached when I had to stop collecting and start writing if a book was to be produced. However, in retrospect, I do feel that it has been my privilege not only to have been able to interview many of our Commonwealth's solid citizens, but also to have talked with some of its unsung heroes. Ranking near the top of this latter category would have to be W. G. Jones of Phillipsburg, Harris Breth of Clearfield, and Professor Sam Bayard of Penn State University.

The late W. G., "Turk", Jones, once described as "The Johnny Appleseed for our time", became, much to his surprise, an international consultant on the methods of reforesting strip-mined lands and soils polluted by mine acids. Owner of Rollingstone Tree Farm, consisting of over twelve-hundred acres of forest land in Clearfield County, Mr. Jones was also an avid teller of the tales of long ago.

To Mr. Breth goes the credit of writing and helping to pass into law, under Governor Earle's administration, some of the state's finest game laws. Also, Breth's popular 1950's television program, "Outdoors With Harris Breth", promoted an awareness of conservation in Pennsylvania. A dedicated hunter and fisherman himself, Mr. Breth had talked first-hand with some of the state's old-time panther and wolf hunters, and even with those who had once been trappers of the passenger pigeon.

The last, but certainly not least, of the aforementioned unsung heroes I spoke with was professor Sam Bayard. Professor Sam spent a lot of time during the 1920's and 1930's collecting traditional fife and fiddle tunes in the mountains of Pennsylvania. His books, *Hill Country Tunes*, and *Dance to the Fiddle, March to the Fife*, are destined to become classics in the field. Bayard's efforts helped preserve the original music once heard in our mountains - Old World ballads brought to this country by early European immigrants. Now adulterated by radio and television, the examples preserved by Sam Bayard could no longer be found today.

Unfortunately, time and distance prevented me from visiting all those who should have been asked to tell their stories. Consequently, it sometimes seemed as though the "Grim Reaper" was just one step ahead of me. I just missed talking to R. Dudley Tonkin, builder of the "last raft" on the Susquehanna, by six months. Likewise, there were those whom I had known in my youth, both my grandfathers for example, that would probably have been rich sources of folk tales had I been interested enough to ask. There were no Civil War veterans around to interview when I did finally get interested enough to start collecting the old tales, but I could have talked to John Bloser, the old Spanish American War vet who lived at the entrance to Decker Valley, Centre County. Travelers passing by his old log cabin could often see the friendly hermit walking around his property, just enjoying the beauty and solitude of the mountains. However, I was drawn to other alluring tales in different areas of the state, and so the old hermit was often seen but never interviewed.

Many other parts of the Commonwealth were visited as much as possible, but certainly not as extensively as desired. Despite the limitations, some traveling was done just for the purpose of collecting stories and tales. In the end, after twenty years of collecting, the territory covered extended from the Grand Canyon of Pennsylvania in the north to the battlefield of Gettysburg in the south, and from the Blue Mountains of the Pennsylvania Dutch country in the east to the Alleghenies and the steel country to the west.

So as time would allow, a large and colorful portion of the state was canvassed in order to find the tales I wanted. As a result, there was a wide variety in both the story types collected and in the backgrounds of the people who were kind enough to tell me their tales. Consequently, I could never predict where I might find myself listening to an account next.

I talked with Clarence Musser in a tent at the "town of tents" - the Centre County Grange Fair and Encampment, held the last week of every August in my home town of Centre Hall. Out in the woods, Roy Corman would talk of the old days as he and my father and

I would tramp through the Seven Mountains during turkey hunting season. Nellie Jack, former resident of the Cornplanter Reservation in Pennsylvania, talked to me in her house on the Seneca Indian Reservation in Salamanca, New York, but Harris Breth and I chatted in a car just outside Clearfield. Other folks were interviewed in barns, antique shops, gas-lit hunting camps, and, in one case, during a break in a graduate school class in New Jersey.

In order to introduce some sort of order to the collection, I've categorized them into six basic types:

1. Stories and Legends About Indians: these are the tales and family traditions that preserve accounts of the Keystone State's Indians.

2. Hunting Tales: stories of the days when "big game" was found in our mountains. Very hard to find anymore, these are the accounts of encounters with wolves and mountain lions, and narratives about the exploits of the big market hunters during the logging era in Pennsylvania.

3. Tales of Everyday Life: these are the stories that convey a picture of what daily life was like in times past. They capture the humor and the pathos of those "Good Old Days".

4. Ghost Stories: a very common tale, even today ghosts seem unaware, or don't care, that we modern and enlightened people no longer believe in them.

5. Witch Tales: not as prevalent as they were fifty years ago, there are still some of the old stories to be found, and also some that are of more recent vintage than most of us would imagine.

6. Supernatural Anecdotes: tales of strange events and weird happenings have always been around. I was able to collect a few - some old, some new; and rather than try to pass judgment on them, I decided to preserve them as told and then try to discover their origins.

This categorization is certainly not the only way the stories can be arranged, but it seems adequate. One thing the reader may notice about the collection is the preponderance of ghost stories, witch tales, and supernatural accounts. I had no intention of emphasizing these types over the other kinds, it just turned out that these seem to be the most common type story that can be collected today. I would have preferred to hear more of the other kinds - particularly the Indian, wolf, and panther stories. However, this imbalance does not seem to be unique to today. There has always been a strong hint of the supernatural in all folklore and legend - a fact that becomes apparent as the origins of the tales in my last volume, in this volume, and in future ones, are revealed.

As for myself, I've always been refreshed and fascinated by the whole project. What could be more enjoyable than visiting those spots whose names or whose legends have evoked pleasant mental images of what might be found there today? What other form of hunting has no season or limits, yet takes one to little-visited corners and nooks where there is yet to be found a vivid picture of the past? There certainly may have been individuals that were better trained and more qualified for this endeavor, but none of them seems to have had the idea of collecting legends and folktales from all over the forgotten byways of the Pennsylvania mountains, and then trying to discover the stories' origins.

In the years to come there may, indeed, be others who also decide to gather the traditions and stories of the long ago, but I believe they will not have the opportunity I have had for rescuing tales on the verge of extinction. There were many old-time episodes still to be found when I first started collecting, but today the unique generation of people who cared about the legends and who had heard them as youngsters is rapidly dwindling, and now it's getting harder to find anyone who grew up in the "horse and buggy days" - that period of time when life and legend somehow seem to have been more romantic and ideal when we look back upon them today, even though reality was something different.

Ideally, there should be no inaccuracies in this or in the previous volume, but they do happen despite efforts. I've tried to be careful about historical facts and sources, but mistakes slip in, as several that exist in the first volume were pointed out to me. There, in my story entitled *Detweiler*, I mention that Alan Seeger was noted for his poems on trees, when, in fact, it was Joyce Kilmer, another World War I doughboy whose forest monument could once be found on Paddy Mountain of Union County. It was also pointed out to me that in the story entitled *Witchmaster versus Witch*, I stated that Fayette County is west of Greene County, when it is the other way around. Hopefully there are no such errors in the present work.

It is with this background, then, that this second volume of Pennsylvania fireside tales is presented for the public's reading enjoyment. As explained in the first volume of this series, the title "fireside tales" comes from the fact that these stories and legends are variants of, or are exactly like, episodes that were related by early settlers sitting around their fireplaces on cold winter evenings when story-telling was the only form of entertainment by which to relax.

Return now to those days of old when the pace was slower and life was harder. Keep in mind, however, that people then seemed content with their lot, finding pleasure in simple things like a wolf's howl, a panther's cry, a firefly's glow, or a flaming sunset sinking slowly behind the everlasting hills.

THE BLACK GHOST OF SCOTIA

Perhaps one of the most unusual geographical landmarks in central Pennsylvania is a vast wasteland in western Centre County that is so inhospitable that nothing of any value seems to grow there. The place is not desolate, but it is rather bleak and barren, almost as though it were cursed by the gods of husbandry. Located about five miles northwest of State College, this infertile section of real estate was first settled by Shawnee Indians who tried to cultivate the land. The acid soil proved too harsh to support agricultural pursuits of any kind, even for the county's native sons, and so the Indians moved on to more productive ground. They did, however, attach a name to the place, probably as a warning to others who might consider farming this territory. Their title has survived even to this day, and almost everyone living within thirty miles of State College has heard of the "Scotia Barrens" - or just "The Barrens", to locals who are really familiar with the place and who don't need to qualify the name assigned by the aborigines.

Decades after the Indians moved away, white settlers began to resettle this section, finding natural resources here that were ideal for their own industries. Consequently, The Barrens became even more desolate-looking as the years went by. Tar pits and charcoal operations seemed to sprout up faster than plants of the edible kind. The area's majestic virgin pine trees, which once thrived on the acid soil, were cut down and used to supply the many charcoal furnaces that were erected here and whose cheery fires glowed continuously, day and night. Despite the advances of the Industrial Revolution, advancements in

1

agricultural science did not reveal any secrets for profitably farming on soils like those found in The Barrens, and so the area seemed to be resolutely determined to yield little or nothing of value to those who dared to coax more than a meagre living from it.

That was soon to change, particularly after the end of the Revolutionary War when large deposits of iron ore were discovered in The Barrens, and mining operations began in earnest. The desolate territory that had once proved so inhospitable, and that had appeared reluctant to support human endeavors of any kind, seemed at last to begrudgingly pour forth its riches upon those who would dig for them.

Vast deposits of iron, like those at The Barrens, did not go unnoticed for long, and in 1880 Andrew Carnegie's steel company began buying up land in the area. Carnegie was thoroughly impressed with the huge deposits of iron that were located around the little community that was then called Forest City. The Pittsburgh steel magnate was so delighted with his "great mountain of ore"[1] that he envisioned a town here that would rival Pittsburgh in its grandeur. Accordingly, Carnegie authorized erection of an ore processing plant, along with company houses that would become the nucleus of the town that he renamed Scotia, after his native Scotland. Soon two neighboring towns, River Hill and Marysville, came into existence as more iron workers moved into the area. During this period of economic good times, the number of people living in and around Scotia peaked at 450 to 500.

Wages at the ore plant were as good, if not better than, other comparable jobs in the county, and so working for a dollar and twenty cents a day seemed to be fair pay to the many mule drivers, miners, engineers, crane operators, water boys, and other employees who worked for Carnegie. Stores opened in Scotia as its population grew, and eventually the town boasted its own grocery store, run by Jeb Bottorf, its own saloon, and Jim Granner's shoemaker's shop. The town also had its cultural refinements in the form of a popular cornet band, which was a particular favorite of Andrew Carnegie.

Good times often come to an end, and Scotia's brief day in the sun eventually faded into dusk as the ore plant became too expensive to operate. Thirty years after they came into existence, the villages of Scotia, River Hill, and Marysville became ghost towns when iron operations closed for good, victim of larger quantities of higher quality ore found along the Great Lakes in Minnesota. The harsh economic realities of the times forced people to leave The Barrens for employment elsewhere, and so the area was left once again to grow up in scrub oak, pitch pine, and similarly-unattractive undergrowth such as hawthorn bushes, poison sumac, and deadly nightshade.

Memories of the old iron ghost towns did last as long as those that had lived there were still alive, but eventually even these recollections faded away as the original inhabitants died off. Junk dealers gradually carted away the machinery that once processed vast quantities of rich iron ore, and wood from some of the houses that were the now-deserted homes of Carnegie employees was used to build barns in the surrounding countryside. In fact, it wasn't too long until only foundations remained to mark the site of this once-thriving boomtown. The Barrens was once again a lifeless place, left to the mercy of its old Nemesis - the forest fires that often swept through the trees, leaving the ground as black as the sable coat of night.

Perhaps these very same fires did more than temporarily blacken the landscape of The Scotia Barrens. Just maybe, if we want to stretch our imaginations a bit, the soot of the infernos darkened a soul as well. More likely, however, the soul of which we speak was as dark as it could get even before the forest fires returned to The Barrens. For there is, according to local legend, a restless ghost that haunts the hills around the old iron ghost towns - a soul that can find no rest due to the dastardly deeds it committed when it was flesh and blood, and which, when it appears to others, manifests itself not as a typical pale spirit, but one whose vapors are the color of soot.

Black clouds did seem to be gathering over the crest of nearby Gatesburg Ridge during the start of Scotia's economic slide in 1910. Even the outlines of the Bald Eagle Mountains to the north must have appeared darker and more foreboding as the harsh realities of the times became apparent. Such periods tend to prey upon men's minds, and this must have been truer as the year wore on, for it was in October of that same year that a sensational murder took place in The Barrens - a murder that would lead to the arrest, conviction, and hanging of a black man named Bert Delige. Delige was no choir boy. He had spent time in prison twice before - once for voluntary manslaughter in western Pennsylvania, and another time for attempted armed robbery at John Haugh's grocery store in Scotia. During this last escapade, Delige had shot at Haugh but had wounded Haugh's nephew, Tom, instead. Now, on this October night in 1910, Delige was about to commit his last crime.

No doubt the October night air was bone-chilling. To this day The Barrens is noted for fall and winter temperatures that can be up to thirty or forty degrees lower than the country around it - a phenomena that's caused by the gradual absorption of cold air by the iron deposits in the ground, which then act like a giant ice cube. But even though the weather was probably very cold, that night in 1910, the heavens above must have been glowing.

One local man, who was in Scotia the night Delige committed his murder, could not forget how well-defined the sky seemed to be. "It was a beautiful moonlit night," recalled Tom McKivison of Bellefonte in 1985. "I don't think I've ever seen it so clear."[2] Perhaps the night was so bright that Mrs. Hulda Baudis, 51-year-old widow of John Baudis, decided it was safe enough to take a short cut when she started to walk back home after a visit with her sister. Her route led past the old mud dam, and though it was a deserted area, Mrs. Baudis probably decided the night air was too cold to walk a longer path. Her decision was a fatal one, for lying in wait in a corn field near her house was a black man who had once worked for her husband, the well-known "merry-go-round man" of Centre County.

Bert Delige claimed that the Baudis's still owed him back wages, but Mrs. Baudis disagreed. Delige had drunk himself into a towering rage that Sunday evening, and, recalled Tom McKivison, "when she got there, he jumped out and raped her. He let her up and started to run off; but she called out that she recognized him and would see that he paid for what he had done. So then Bert, he just wheeled around and caught her and cut her throat with his razor."[2]

It took nearly six months before Bert Delige paid for his crime, despite the overwhelming evidence against him. Footprints in the mud at the murder scene matched Bert's shoes exactly. The clothing he had worn that night was splattered with what appeared to be blood stains. Many witnesses stated that Delige was intoxicated the night of the crime. Other witnesses testified that they saw the suspect lingering around the mud dam on that same evening. Then, about a month later, a Pinkerton detective found a blood-spattered razor hidden under some leaves near the Delige home. It took a jury about four hours before deciding that Delige was guilty, and once the all-male jury delivered the verdict, it took another week before Judge Ellis Orvis decided upon the sentence - death by hanging.

As Bert Delige's execution date drew near, the public interest in the affair grew more intense. There had not been as much excitement about a public execution since Ira Green and William Dillen were publicly hung in the Bellefonte jail yard six years before. Dillen and Green had killed Jerry Condo, the turnkey at the Centre County prison, during a prison break one summer night in 1904. That same evening the people of Bellefonte were being serenaded by a cornet band - not the Forest City Cornet Band from The Scotia Barrens, but a cornet band just the same; this one from Coleville. Ten months later people streamed into Bellefonte to be "entertained" by the hangings that took place in front of a crowd that grew to about 750 as the scheduled executions approached. It was a spectacle which many people wanted to see. Excitement reached a fever pitch around 10:30 on the morning of May ninth when the two murderers were led into the jail yard and up the double scaffold. The crowd grew quiet when bags were placed over the men's heads and nooses were slipped around their necks. With that, one of the condemned men turned to the other and said, "Well, here we go."[3]

Eventually peoples' appetites for violent scenes like the public hangings of Dillen and Green diminished, but that change was a gradual one, and it wasn't until 1915 that Pennsylvania adopted the electric chair as its accepted method of execution. Consequently, public hangings continued for some time in Centre County, and Bert Delige's execution was to be an affair that some probably thought would be as well-attended as the hangings of Dillen and Green. However, the afternoon that Delige was hung, April 25, 1911, a crowd of just sixty people came to see the event - far fewer than the hundreds that made such a mad scramble to get in to see Dillen and Green hung that "hats were crushed and lost, and clothing torn"[4].

Delige's hanging went off without incident, and his body was taken back to The Barrens and interred in non-hallowed ground. Instead of being buried in the nearby negro cemetery - segregation was even a practice that applied to the dead in those days - Delige's corpse was placed in a grave near the Delige homestead. No service was conducted, and a simple, unmarked, flat stone was placed over the internment site. That seemed to settle the matter once and for all, and people knew that justice had been served. However, even though the public mind was satisfied, it would seem, if local folktales are any basis for reaching such conclusions, that the indestructible part of Bert Delige, what some would call his spiritual essence, was not.

Sixty-six years after Bert Delige was hung in the Bellefonte jail yard, a carload of deer hunters decided to drive through the Scotia Barrens one night to spot-light deer. Hoping to see some nice-looking bucks that would make impressive trophies come hunting season, the Nimrods instead saw something that would make them scratch their heads for weeks. It was not the type of thing that some of them could forget, and one of the men mentioned the episode when he stopped in at the Bellefonte Library shortly after the sighting occurred. The woman behind the counter knew nothing about Scotia, nor about its history, but Hugh Manchester, that indefatigable historian of the Bellefonte region, was standing nearby and overheard the conversation.

"This started to go through my mind," recalled Mr. Manchester in a 1981 recording session. "And then I introduced myself. He stressed there were four or five men with him. They had just gone out to spot deer or something. Then they saw this big black image coming toward them. It wasn't a black cloud. It was a human being -

7

I mean it gave the appearance, but it was over-sized. They were stunned by it. So they had told their wives about it, and they were going back.

"I kept the specifics to myself, and I didn't tell him the background. I said, 'When were you there?' And he said, 'On the evening of April 25th'. And then, you know, right away I think, 'Oh my God, that's the day they hanged Bert Delige.'

"And I said, 'Where specifically did this happen?'. And he described it, and this was the place where she [Mrs. Baudis] had been murdered."[5]

Folklore says that there are a number of things that don't allow a departed soul to find its eternal peace, among them being the lack of a proper burial. Another is the urge to atone for a wrong done when the spirit was in human form. Either of these could apply to Bert Delige's immortal soul, but his restless spirit, if, indeed, there is a restless shade, should be content in one respect at least. Bert Delige was the last man to be publicly hung in Centre County. That surely closes one chapter in the annals of Pennsylvania criminology. However, oddly enough, that same chapter started and ended with similar characters. It turns out that the first man publicly hung in Centre County was also a black murderer.

The very first capital crime in Centre County occurred in 1802 when a black man named Daniel Byers ambushed another black man named James Barrows. The shooting, which took place close to the Valentine Iron Works near Bellefonte, was inspired by a feud over a woman. Byers was easily convicted of the murder, and James Duncan, high sheriff of Centre County, was ordered to hang him publicly. On the 13th of December, 1802, a large crowd of "forgemen and other original characters"[6] gathered around the hangman's scaffolding to witness the execution. The trapdoor of the scaffolding opened as it should have, but on Dan's first swing the rope broke. Byers landed on the ground without being hurt, and the crowd thought he should go free. However, the hapless murderer was led back up the scaffolding and was "hung like a man."[6]

Unlike Dan Byers, Bert Delige didn't have to be hung twice to pay for his crime. However, folklore seems to indicate that Bert Delige's ultimate penalty was harsher than Byers'. At least that would probably be the conclusion of those who have actually seen the swirling black mist that appears near the site of the old mud dam on those nights of April twenty-fifth when the sky is crystal clear and the moon casts a ghostly light on the lonesome shadows of The Scotia Barrens.

FOOTNOTE: Almost all of the Scotia Barrens are now preserved as state game lands, but the towns of Marysville and Scotia have become inhabited again in recent years. The flat stone that once marked Bert Delige's grave has been removed, either by someone who didn't know why it was there, or by a morbid curiosity-seeker. However, the foundation of what was probably the Baudis home can still be seen near where Meeks Lane and Sky Top Lane merge. Largely overgrown with brush and small trees, the foundation is rapidly disappearing and will soon be just another shadowy memory of the tragedy that once occurred here.

The Mud Dam

Scotia Barrens, Centre County

JUNIATA GAP

During the more barbarous times in ancient Europe, when brute force was held to be one of the most respected measures of a man, the kings and warriors of that age often had names that included the word "wolf". The reasoning, or hope, leading to this practice was that by using the word wolf as part of one's name that person might also acquire some of the wolf's qualities; and so names like Ethelwulf ("the Nobel Wolf") and Ealdwulf ("the Old Wolf") appear in the histories of those days.[1] It was, of course, the wolf's audacity and ferocity that a barbarian would admire most - the same qualities that a warrior would want in order to stimulate terror in his enemies. Wolves were a common worry in almost every European country in ancient times. These fearless predators would often attack solitary travelers, and, when hungry enough, were even known to enter towns in search of prey. Because of these cold-hearted and bloodthirsty actions, wolves were marked for extermination.

Everyone was encouraged to kill as many wolves as possible, regardless of how it was done. Eventually all kinds of tactics were employed, including setting whole tracts of forest land on fire just to burn the grey marauders to death. Wolves were placed totally outside the protection of any laws, and it was from this fact that a human outlaw, being outside the protection of the law as well, was referred to as a "wolf's-head" by the Saxons of England. In the minds of those early Englishmen, the criminal of that day was just as condemned as a wolf and was just as likely to be killed.

There were few reasons why people of that era would want to keep any wolf alive. Left unchecked, the beasts could become

11

unbelievably bold. Around 1600 in Ireland, for example, hunters had failed to thin the wolf population sufficiently, and their numbers increased dramatically. The result was that "on winter nights they will come and prey in villages and the suburbs of cities".[2] The merciless beasts not only hassled the living but also would not let the dead rest either. In Scotland's Edderachillis District it is recalled that "wolves were at one time so numerous that to avoid their ravages in disintering bodies from their graves, the inhabitants were obliged to have recourse to the island of Handa as a safer place of sepulture." And, "In Athole it was formerly the custom to bury the dead in coffins made of five flagstones to preserve the bodies from Wolves."[3]

Here in Pennsylvania, the wolf behaved much in the same way, roaming the forests almost at will, even after the end of the Civil War. In Perry County, wolves were so bad that "even the graves had to be covered with stones in early times to insure their safety from these animals."[4] Fishing Creek Valley was a favorite haunt of Perry County's wolves, and in that same county there is a narrow defile on Mt. Patrick known as "The Narrows" which, at one time, was also regarded as a particularly dangerous spot due to its many wolf dens. Moreover, on the Perry County ridge still known as Crawley Hill, in Spring Township, there is a small collection of boulders, rising to about a height of fifteen feet, that was once known as 'the wolf rocks'. The name, according to tradition, arose from the fact that this was a spot where wolves would often rendezvous.

Now we can only imagine what unearthly sounds the beasts must have made as they stood upon the rocks and howled at the misty yellow moon before embarking on one of their nocturnal hunts. It was the type of music that must have sent chills up the spine of even the most fearless backwoodsman. Today the rocks on Crawley Hill no longer serve as a home for wolves. Foxes now make good use of the boulders, selecting them for their own natural dens.

Perry County wasn't exceptional when it came to wolfish inhabitants. Wolves were a plague to the residents of other counties as well. Centre County raftsmen who floated arks down Penns Creek from Coburn to Selinsgrove and then walked back through the mountains often encountered them, but no stories of wolf attacks on the raftsmen have come down to us over the years. Up in the Black Forest counties of Elk, Potter, Tioga, and others in this northern tier, wolves were a common nuisance and were not brought under control until almost the turn of the last century. However, even though the wolf was an ever-present threat to humans, it was not this alone, or even this primarily, that doomed him to extinction. Economics was the driving force behind the wolf's demise, just as it was in Europe. In both places wolves created financial headaches by killing off a farmer's livestock.

Sheep, in particular, were a favorite prey of wolves, a preference that made it "a hard matter in those days to raise sheep on account of the mountain prowling wolves who were a menace to the early settlers."[5] In fact, in this country, from 1682 to 1705, wolves "continued to increase so that sheep raising became almost impossible."[6] It was for this reason that generous bounties were offered for every wolf a person could kill. Some people even became professional wolf hunters, earning more money in this way than they could have earned just as common laborers.

Wolf hunting was a dangerous profession, and one which was not for the faint-hearted. One man, who encountered many wolves during his early hunting days in Pennsylvania, explained it this way: "I have listened in my bed to the dismal howl of the wolf, and for the benefit of those who never heard a wolf's musical soiree I will state here

13

that one wolf leads off in a long tenor, and then the whole pack joins in the chorus. A small pack of half a dozen wolves will make the mountain seem alive for miles. The cry is anything but reassuring to the timid soul who is shut in safely by the fire of his forest cabin. It is enough to chill the marrow of the man who for the first time hears it when he is in the unprotected open."[7]

The same old wolf hunter, commenting on the "vicious and savage" nature of the beasts, also states that, in his opinion, it is hunger that gives them their courage and which drives them to desperate acts. "That is why," he notes, "the wolf is such a ferocious enemy when once he is aroused to attack man. Death by starvation is no more alluring to him than death by the hand of his possible prey."[7]

Perhaps the wolf was not as unconcerned with death as the previous description may indicate. Oftentimes a wolf's prey would be weaker animals like sheep and deer, and even then the wolf would not, at least in the case of deer, attack singly, preferring to hunt in packs instead. They would hunt deer in this way until they flushed one out. The entire pack would chase the deer until they were tired, at which point a lone wolf would continue the chase at full tilt. The rest of the pack would rest and watch while the lone wolf would try to circle the deer back around to them. Once the deer was directed past the waiting pack, one or two rested wolves would take up the chase. This alternation of pursuing wolves would continue until the deer was too tired to run anymore, at which time it would head for the nearest stream. A line of wolves would then form on each side of the stream next to the deer. At this point there was no escape, and "the deer would become an easy prey to these ravenous creatures."[8]

A lone wolf would attack a sheep, however, and could "seize it by the throat and throw it over on his back"[9], sometimes carrying it this way for a distance of several miles. It was because of a sheep's great vulnerability to wolf attacks that the husbandmen of those times would often tie bells around the necks of their sheep as well as their cattle. This was a common practice in those early days, as described by Rev. Philip Fithian as he passed through the West Branch Valley in 1775. Traveling through a calm and luxuriant woods one evening at sunset, the time of day poets would call "the golden hour" a hundred years later, Fithian was struck by the melodious sounds of bells. Bells "tinkling from every quarter", and fastened around the necks of grazing sheep and horses and also around the necks of cows heading back to their barns for the night. He would later write that the sounds were "a continued and cheering echo" that turned the silence of the forest into "a transporting vesper."[10]

The following folktale also preserves the memory of the bells once placed around sheep's necks. The story shows, too, the main reason they were placed there and points out the fact that wolves not only attacked flocks, but also weren't shy about turning on herdsmen as well. It's an interesting episode from the Allegheny Mountains of Blair County, recalled by a fine old gentleman who was almost two years past the century mark when he related the tale to me.

"Nathaniel Maurer was my uncle," began the old miner. "He lived in Morrison's Cove at one time, where he kept a flock of sheep. He also lived in Juniata Gap at another time; that's now part of Altoona. Sheep were good bait for wolves in those days, but the wolves never lasted long because the old people always killed one when they saw it. They'd hunt by forming a circle to surround panthers and wolves; then they'd close in and kill them.

"My uncle could always tell when the wolves were bothering his sheep because he would hear the bells around the sheep's necks tinkling more than usual. One afternoon, when he was living at Juniata Gap, he heard these bells and figured that the wolves were probably after his sheep. He started for the field and took his rifle with him. When he got to the field, a wolf that was hiding in some high grass lunged at him. He was so surprised that he only had time to throw up his rifle between himself and the wolf.

"The wolf bit into the wooden stock of the rifle and its two long front teeth put two scratch marks across it. It just gave my uncle time enough to bring the rifle around and shoot the wolf. This happened within two-hundred yards of the old Maurer graveyard at Juniata Gap. He always tanned all the hides he could get his hands on, so he probably tanned this wolf's hide too. He had five guns he kept in his house, and they all burned up, along with all his wolf hides and the gun with the tooth marks on the stock, when his house burned down. That gun sure would have been a relic today."[11]

The circle or "ring" hunts mentioned by the old gentleman were once a common method of hunting game. Nonetheless, it was not a very safe way of hunting, and so it's not done today, probably dying out shortly after the howl of the wolf disappeared from the lonesome valleys where its songs were once commonplace. However, ring hunts and Nathaniel Maurer's tooth-marked rifle are not the only links with the Pennsylvania wolf that have disappeared over the years.

Many of the old beliefs and superstitions associated with the wolf have also faded away. The Indians used to believe, for example, that if a wolf barked at a person it was a sign the person would have a long life. They also believed that wolves would howl when there was a change coming in the weather. Whites, too, had their superstitions about the wolf, including a belief that "Whoever carries the right eye of a wolf fastened inside of his right sleeve, remains free from all injury".[12]

There were, however, some tangible things that men found useful about the wolf. In England, for example, the medicinal properties of the mineral waters at Bath were discovered by someone's noticing that cattle which had been attacked by wolves always headed directly for the waters at Bath. The wounded animals would stand in the refreshing waters, instinctively seeming to know that they were being helped. Afterwards they would always heal sooner and better than they would by any other applications. Then, too, Indians and whites alike seemed to find some utility in displaying different bodily parts of the wolf. Captain John Smith of the Colony of Virginia is credited with being the first white man to see the Indians of Pennsylvania, and his description of the Susquehannock Indians in 1608 mentions that their attire was wolf and bear skins. He goes on to say that one of the Susquehannocks had a necklace with a wolf's head serving as its decoration.

Much like the Indian who used the wolf's head as a jewel or good luck charm, many white settlers had a custom of nailing wolf paws on their barns for good luck. After the wolves had been exterminated in Pennsylvania, and wolf paws could no longer be obtained to nail onto barns, the legs and claws of wild turkeys were used instead. This is still a custom that can be found today at some hunting camps. One such camp, still in use today, sits on Nittany Mountain, Centre County, where two or three wild turkey legs and claws are prominently displayed on the front of the cabin. Perhaps the legs are placed there today for good luck or perhaps just as evidence of a successful hunting season. In any case, the hunters who place them there probably don't realize that the practice dates back to earlier times when there were wolves in these same woods, and that the placement of those turkey legs may be one of the last surviving customs linking the modern day to those times when the call of a wolf on a cold winter night was enough to send a lone hunter scurrying back to his cabin to sit safely beside the warmth of a cheery fire crackling in his fireplace.

The Wolf Rocks

Crawley Hill, Perry County

(Where the wolves used to howl in the old days)

THROUGH THE VEIL

Soothsayers and tokens (signs of things to come), have always been a source of fascination to many people at one time or another, and here in Pennsylvania there are quite a few stories dealing with these types of individuals and events. Such tales can be a real source of entertainment for those who are intrigued by the possibility that our futures can be seen in advance, thereby warning us of imminent danger or revealing the consequences of certain actions. There are, in fact, many people who think that peeking "through the veil" that separates the present from the future is entirely possible. There are many others who not only believe that such foresight is feasible, but also base that conviction on personal experiences. This is certainly not a belief that is new to the twentieth century. It is a concept that stretches back to at least medieval times or beyond. In other words, there have probably been fortunetellers around for as long as there have been civilizations. Likewise, the belief in portents and signs has probably been around for just as long, if not longer.

One of the oldest Pennsylvania stories dealing with a personal token was related by Mary Jemison, the fifteen-year-old Scotch-Irish maiden with the golden hair, who was abducted from her parents' house in Buchanan Valley, Adams County, by a party of French and Indians in 1758. She would later recall that the day before her kidnapping and her parents' murders, she was sent to a neighbor's house, about a mile away, to procure a horse and spend the night. On her way that evening, she saw what appeared to be an outspread sheet coming toward her. The sheet seemed to close around her, and she lost consciousness. Her neighbors found her, and they took her back to their house, where they applied some tried-and-true home remedies to revive her, but were unable to do so until the next morning. Mary quickly regained her good health and was able to return home immediately, only to be captured by the Indian raiding party that would later kill her parents and take her on to the Genessee Valley of New York. The remainder of her life she would spend with the Indians, and during that time the "white woman of the Genesee", as she became known, strongly believed that the strange sheet-like form was a token of the "melancholy catastrophe" that befell her family. She also believed that her envelopment by the sheet was a token of her "preservation from death at the time we were captured."[1]

If Mary Jemison was ever forewarned of future events again, she at least did not mention it in depositions of her interesting life. However, in past years there have been other Pennsylvanians who seem to have had the future revealed to them as well. For instance, Henry Voneida of eastern Penns Valley, Centre County, had a reputation as a seer during the second half of the last century. One of his most famous predictions concerned the airplane, which would not be invented until 1903. One day as he sat twiddling his thumbs, this old Pennsylvania Dutchman stated, "Die cite comed woe die lied ind die loft rom flige in alle die machine dos glebbert die in alle die dresh machine und monicer ford ins hellveter nie." (The day will come when man will fly in the air in an old machine that rattles like an old threshing machine, and many will fly in thunderstorms). [2]

Although the average person doesn't have insights like Mary Jemison or Henry Voneida, there are those who once thought that they had methods to help peer through the misty portals of time. However, as readers of my first book will realize, these were not new tools. Their origins were rooted somewhere in the dim past, especially the methods used to divine who, or what sort of person, one's mate would be. During the mid-1800's in Lancashire, England, for example, one of the popular practices around New Year's Day was for single girls to pour a small amount of molten lead into a glass of water. Any young lady interested in knowing the occupation of her future husband would play this game, peering intently into the water to see what shape the drops of lead formed as they landed on the bottom of the glass. If they appeared to be like scissors, then the young lady expected she would marry a tailor; a hammer meant a blacksmith or a carpenter, and so on. However, such practices were not confined to Europe. In this country even the Indians apparently had their own methods for divining their future mates.

In her interesting book entitled *Folk Medicine of the Delaware*, Gladys Tantaquidgeon says that, according to the folk beliefs of the Delaware and related Algonkian Indians, there were several ways that a person could find out who their intended was to be. It's not really clear whether these might have been ideas that the Indians adopted from the white man, but it would seem likely this is the case. Either way, it is certain that the notions have old origins. One such idea had it that a young girl could see the image of her future husband by taking a mirror to a well at noon on the first day of May. She was to then hold the mirror over the well so the reflection of the water was captured in the looking glass. If she did all this correctly, so said the old belief, then her future mate's image should appear in the mirror as well.

According to the same source, Delaware Indian maidens had one other method for discovering the identity of their future husbands. This, too, was probably a practice that the Indians learned from the white race, but it's roots must have been deep ones also. The belief here was that the girl should first take two balls of yarn and tie

22

their ends together. She was then to find an old deserted house with a second story and throw one ball of yarn out an upstairs window while holding the other ball. The young lady was then to say, "I wind my yarn. Who'll wind agin' me?"[3] Her intended husband would, it was believed, then come, as if drawn by some supernatural power, and pick up the ball of yarn that had been thrown out the window.

These "Delaware" convictions certainly sound more like white men's notions, but whether or not the Indians gave the beliefs to the whites or the other way around, the ideas seemed to last a long time. People in western Pennsylvania's Greene County, for example, were still familiar with them in the early decades of this century.

"A prevalent belief there at one time was that if you threw a ball of yarn into a haunted house while holding on to the end of the string ,you could then say 'I wind, I wind. Who holds?', explained the well-known folklorist. "Supposedly, the ghost in the house would then reveal the name of the one you were to marry."

"John Meighen lived in Wind Ridge or Jacktown, Greene County, back in the 1930's," continued the professor. "He was an old-time fiddler, and one day he was sitting on his front porch playing his fiddle when several young boys stopped to talk. They told him they were going to try out this idea about the yarn in an old, reputedly haunted, house down the road. And, of course, John slipped into the house, the deserted house, being aware of their plans. He sneaked down the hillside and hid in there. When they threw in the ball of yarn and chanted 'I wind, I wind. Who holds?', he called out the name of some very low-repute girl in the neighborhood. This really shook them up, you know. The were very downcast, and then they began to get suspicious, and they entered the house. But, of course, by that time John was out, and he sneaked his way up through the bushes and up the hillside. When they came up again, full of mystification, he was sitting on the front porch playing his fiddle, and never let on."[4]

Another way folks down in Greene County once believed they could find out who they were to marry was by having a meal called a "dumb dinner." "The people would make a dinner," continued the professor, "and it would be heavily salted. No one dared to speak, and the idea was that if no one spoke, the person whom someone in the group was destined to marry would come in and join them for dinner. Otherwise, they would see them in a dream that night after the dinner."[4]

Many, if not all, of these quaint ideas about tokens and signs were transplants - ideas brought to this country from the "ould sod", a name early immigrants to Pennsylvania sometimes used when referring to their European homeland. Of course, many of these immigrants were lured here to the Keystone State in hopes of finding jobs, including employment in the bituminous and anthracite mines of Pennsylvania's coal regions. These newcomers came from all over Europe, but most of the original miners in Pennsylvania were English, Welsh, Scottish, or Irish. In one sense, then, the mines were "melting pots" where diverse European cultures were blended into what one historian has called "the American, this new man".[5]

Despite the molding of so many different backgrounds into one homogeneous society, there were still beliefs and ideas that were unique to the countries from which these transplanted people had come. Some of these notions from the "Old Country" gradually disappeared as the years rolled by; but others were more persistent, taking longer to die and lasting well into the middle of the twentieth century. Included in this long-lasting group was a quaint, others may say frightening, belief from St. Patrick's island - an entity the Irish called a banshee.

24

Some Irish legends declared that the banshee was a female fairy that haunted desolate spots in the forests or little-traveled back-roads through the hills. Also said to be the disembodied spirits of former relations or of departed family friends, banshees supposedly singled out that household as the one they would warn when a family death was imminent. This was accomplished, so said the mystical stories from the Emerald Isle, through nocturnal visits characterized by blood-curdling screams and weird, mournful, wails that left little doubt as to their meaning.

The old Irish legends even provided a portrait of these fanciful harbingers of death, describing them as beautiful blonde maidens or as ugly old hags, depending on whether their warnings were soft and comforting or hateful and terrifying. It was also believed at one time that the banshees gave their warnings several days in advance, thereby allowing the doomed to prepare themselves for passage to the next realm and also giving relatives time to adjust to the loss they were about to experience. Not ones to migrate from their native soil, banshees stayed behind when family members emigrated to America. However, if an old family tradition from Luzerne County is to be believed, the banshees never lost track of anyone.

"Sometime in the mid or late 1800's, my grandfather and grandmother both came over here from County Mayo Ireland," recalled the coal miner's grandson. "My grandfather was Jim McCabe, and his two brothers, Will and Ted, came with him. There was Jim, Ted, and Bill - they called him Will. It was Will that got killed here.

"Will was the one that died here in America, and by the time the letter got back to Ireland, a letter was already back over here telling that they knew about it. He worked for Keyhoe-Berge Coal Company; in the early 30's I think it was. He got off of work, and they were bringing the miners out of the hole. He was down in the mine, in the shaft, waiting for the ride to come up. And one of the workers that got off must've hit a little stone, and the little stone fell down the shaft and hit him in the head. It might've fallen a couple of hundred feet, you know."

"That evening in Ireland, banshees appeared in front of Will's father's house, crying and going on, and in a loud voice said 'Will McCabe is dead in America.' At the time, Will was in his early fifties. A telegram arrived at my grandfather's house, about the same time their telegram arrived in Ireland proclaiming Will's death. Now the telegram from Ireland to the United States was dated the day after Will's death, and it stated that they knew Will was dead through the word of the banshees and that a 'wake' was held for him in Ireland."

Continuing on with the story his grandmother had once related to him, the miner's grandson had more to tell about Irish banshees. "Yeah, all the dogs in the area started howling," he continued. "And then these old women would come. They were called banshees. They would all dress in black. They would start crying and howling, you know, and mourning. One of them said that Will was dead in America. They'd only spend about an hour or so, and they'd mourn."[6]

So whether it was through banshees, "dumb" dinners, balls of yarn, or mirrors, there were ways, some Pennsylvanians once thought, that the future was ours to know. However, whether or not that future was something worth knowing would most certainly depend on what was supposedly revealed, and, most people would likely agree, how it was revealed. Not too many people are interested in finding out what lies in store for them anyway, and, indeed, lots of us would probably be glad to remain ignorant rather than be awakened some foggy night by the wails of those mythical Irish maidens that were called banshees.

SNAKES, SNAKES, SNAKES

Many people would number snakes among the things that they abhor the most. Even the smallest of these beneficial reptiles is enough to cause a lot of individuals to feel pangs of horror if they happen to get close to one. It's little wonder, then, that normal-sized snakes are feared even more by those who don't want anything at all to do with slithering animals of any kind. It is these types of fears that are projected, I think, into the exaggerated snake stories that are found in folktales. What better way to convey an irrational, overwhelming, fear of snakes than to create a tall-tale that describes them as larger than life? Following are several such Pennsylvania mountain stories that once provided favorite topics when story tellers spun their yarns around the pot-bellied stoves of old country stores.

"Log" Snakes > > > > > > > > > > > > >

Up in the northeastern Pennsylvania coal country, around the end of the nineteenth century, there was once a tale about a man who made a living by hauling wagon-loads of charcoal from the Pocono Mountains to an iron furnace in Lehigh County. "Old man" Snyder, it was said, would often recount a strange experience he had one exceptionally hot day while driving his team. The day was so hot, in fact, that he was afraid for his horses, and so pulled under a large shady oak tree to give them a rest. Feeling hot and tired himself, he got off his wagon and sat down upon a huge log by the side of the road. Soon he dozed off, lulled into unconsciousness by the hot summer air.

"When he awoke he felt that the log was moving, and that his body leaned downhill," relates the once-popular yarn. The perplexed man immediately jumped off the log and tried to get his bearings, but he couldn't see a trace of the road he had been on before he dozed off, nor could he see his horses. He seemed to be in the middle of dense underbrush or a thicket. Out of the corner of his eye he saw something that just stuck out of the underbrush about half a mile away; whatever it was appeared to be moving. "He saw that it was the head of an immense snake," concludes the folktale - "a snake as thick as a century old tree. He had mistaken the snake for a log and had sat on it, and while he slept it had carried him fully five miles away from his team."[1]

Such tall-tales must have been quite prevalent in the heart of the Pennsylvania "Dutch" country years ago, for there were still versions of the yarn that could be heard in the Blue Mountains of Berks County in 1989. According to a very "Dutchified" Pennsylvania Dutchman, his grandfather had told him about an incident which he claimed happened to him personally.

"Up on a back road there was a bake oven through the woods; this was up near Landis Store," explained the Berks County native with a heavy Pennsylvania Dutch accent. "He came through there with a horse and wagon - a topped buggy, in other words, you know. And the snake was as thick as a stove pipe. Knowing him, I think it was true. And this snake was laying across the road. It was staying in the lime, where they made lime; you know, the old limekilns they had all over. And he couldn't get the horse to cross over this snake. And he kept beatin' the horse to cross over this snake. And he kept beatin' the horse, you know, and finally the horse jumped.

"And when the horse jumped and went over, the snake flipped up and broke the spoke in the wheel. Well, he told me that; that was a big snake, evidently.

"Now I, myself, up at Landis Store - now they told me this and I didn't believe it. I know the area. I don't want'a go up. I bet there were two hundred black snakes layin' on the rocks in this area. It's a black snake den, in other words. It's full of rocks in there. I went in and I seen it. It shook me. I didn't want'a go back."[2]

Snake Eyes > > > > > > > > > > > > > > > >

Rattlesnakes and copperheads are the two poisonous varieties of snakes found in Pennsylvania, and so these two are the most feared. However, even the lowly black snake has gained a reputation as an aggressive reptile to be avoided. This reputation is not without foundation, as anyone who has come face-to-face with a black snake in the woods can probably testify. And the term "face-to-face" is not used loosely here. Black snakes will rise up, not unlike a cobra, and hiss at an intruder. I've personally witnessed this disquieting behavior first-hand, as did one Berks County hiker who didn't stand around wondering what to do next.

"We were going through a field of dead big grass, you know," explained the hiker, "and evidently I stepped on these. They were mating - two black snakes. I didn't measure them, but I know they were high enough to look me right in the face. They stood up and the boys said they never saw anybody take such big steps in their life. I went out'a there like I was floatin', I guess. Scared the [stuff] out of me."[2]

It may be that tales of enormous snakes arose in part from the black snake's trait of making itself look huge by extending its neck and body into the air. It is true, however, that snakes can grow to some pretty impressive lengths, given the right conditions. Maybe those conditions don't exist anymore, here in our Pennsylvania mountains, but they must have been prevalent in Huntingdon County in 1897. According to a Huntingdon County news account, John P. Swoope killed six snakes on Warrior Ridge in July of that year, "the smallest, seven feet 10 inches, and the largest, eleven feet six inches."[3] The account goes on to state that, although the lengths may seem unbelievable, there were undoubtedly old-timers that could testify to having seen snakes of such lengths in the Raystown country during their lifetimes. Anyone can easily imagine the impression an eleven foot snake might create if it raised itself up into a standing position. Trapper Swoope seems to have had just such a thing happen to him. One of the snakes he killed on Warrior Ridge in July of 1897, "ran at me with its head raised about four feet, but I always carry a good stick and took him one on the fly and laid him low."[3]

Given the size (average length is five feet) and actions of the black snake, it is no wonder that there were many superstitions connected with it. Down in Montgomery County a tale was once told about a squirrel hunter who had shot at, but failed to hit, a number of squirrels that he spotted in the trees along Perkiomen Creek.

Just as he was raising his gun to try one more time, he noticed an enormous black snake curled up on the ground nearby. It's steely eyes seemed to be locked upon him in a steady stare. Then, so goes this yarn, he "instinctively knew that he had to do with a power that was protecting the woods and he left off hunting, and went home." The story ends by concluding that the hunter thought that his gun had been charmed by the snake, and that he would soon suffer the same fate if he stayed there.[4]

Such tales were not confined to the eastern part of the state. Way out in Greene County there were similar accounts that once made the rounds there - especially those dealing with huge black snakes and their habit of standing up and looking an intruder right in the eye.

"I did hear stories about enormous black snakes, a foot between the eyes," noted the folklorist. "They would be seen in berry patches, rearing themselves up and looking at the pickers. Rearing their heads up and looking at the people picking the berries."[5]

Milking Snakes > > > > > > > > > > >

Despite their unsavory reputations, black snakes could not have been universally feared. In fact, some people found them useful. Black snakes are excellent "mousers"; even better, it is said, than cats. "These old people all had their snakes pretty well in their houses; black snakes, in the barn or in the house," explained one man. "They would catch mice - mice and rats."[7]

"They'd live in the house in the winter and then they'd be out in the garden in the summertime," explained another.[8]

Perhaps because people saw them so often around their barns and houses it was only natural for black snakes to become part of rural folklore: "Did you ever hear of a black snake milking a cow?", asked a farmer who had heard such tales when he was younger. "They used to claim a black snake could milk a cow," he recalled.[8]

Once again, such tales were not unknown as far west as Greene County, where "The kids used to tell me that if you killed a snake, the cows would give bloody milk," stated the professor. "Which," he offered, "struck me as an extraordinarily bawled up version of an idea that the snakes will milk cows and cause them to give bloody milk."[5]

Now zoologists will tell you that snakes can't suck. In order to drink, a snake must submerge its head in a liquid and then open its

32

mouth to let the water flow in. Moreover, black snakes have sharp teeth that would cause a lot of discomfort to a cow's tender teats. Nonetheless, reports of snakes milking cows have not disappeared over the years, and at least one person claims to have seen it happen. Perhaps, there is something to it after all. Even if the snake gets no milk out of the act, it might think it is going to get a meal if it hangs on long enough. At least this could be the explanation for what a Centre County man says he witnessed in his own barn one morning.

"I'll tell you what I did see one time when we lived down here on the farm," said the retired farmer. "We had one cow and every morning that cow would have no milk in a couple tits. One morning I went out, and there was a snake up there. She laid down and let that snake suck her. That I saw. Yes sir. My wife can tell you. Yes sir, that snake would suck that cow. She'd lay down there and let that snake, yes sir. That I seen with my own eyes, down there when I farmed."[9]

Hoop Snakes > > > > > > > > > > > > > >

Besides the stories about snakes that milk cows and snakes that are as big as logs, there were also tales of snakes that move around in extraordinary ways. Back in the 1930's, kids were oftentimes told scary anecdotes about the blue racer, a snake that was said to be faster than a race horse, and which would squeeze, then eat, any person it could catch. However, the most common story of snakes with extraordinary means of locomotion was that of the hoop snake. Such tales were once common up in Lehigh County, including the following one which was preserved by early collectors Thomas Brendle and "Pumpernickel Bill" Troxell.

According to their version, there was once a farmer who was so tired of his many misfortunes that he would have committed suicide if it weren't for the fact that he thought it to be such a great sin. Resigned to a life of misery, the farmer stoically continued to scratch out a meagre living. Then, "one day he took his hoe and went out into the field to hoe the few stalks of corn that had come up from his planting and had been spared by the blackbirds and the crows. As he hoed he came across a great rattlesnake. 'Let it bite me,' he thought, 'then my troubles will be over.'

"The snake struck, but instead of striking the man it hit the hoe, and then, strange to relate, the handle of the hoe began to swell. It swelled and swelled. Soon it was as thick as a rail; then as a post; then as a log; and finally as the trunk of a great tree. The man, feeling that luck had at last come his way, rolled the log to the saw mill, and had enough shingles cut from the log to cover all his buildings. From that time on he prospered."[10]

Brendle and Troxell went on to note that this was a common story, "founded on an old belief that there is a snake with a horned tale, called 'die Hannschlang."[10] The belief was that this horn-tailed serpent could put its tail in its mouth and form a hoop. It would then roll merrily along through the woods until it ran into a tree. This collision would cause the snake to release its tail, which would imbed itself into the trunk, causing the tree to die.

Although no one believes in hoop snakes anymore, the old folks still remember the stories. Belief in the existence of such snakes may have been widespread at one time, but the tales eventually became nothing more than entertainment or ploys that were used to frighten or impress children. The next two variations are probably good examples of both types of stories. The first version is attributed to

Harold "Bud" Schenck, who told the story in Milt Kunes' general store at Blanchard, Centre County, about seventy-five years ago. The setting for the tale was Chancey Delong's Mill Brook Farm near Blanchard. The corn field is now under the waters of Sayers Dam.

"Bud was hoeing corn in late July," recalled Schenck's friend Bill Davy, who heard Mr. Schenck tell the tale at the store. "The corn was three feet high. He looked up the corn row next to the one he was working in, and here came this hoop snake rolling down the row toward him. About one foot of the hoop snake was above the corn, and he could see the horn or stinger on the snake's tail. He moved over in the next row to let the snake pass. In doing so the snake hit the hoe handle with its stinger or horn, and in five minutes time the handle turned as blue as indigo and swelled up to the size of a stovepipe.

"I didn't see this," explained Davy, "but Mr. Schenck did. And if he says so, that is good enough for me."[11]

It seems that those claiming to have seen fantastic snakes like the log or hoop varieties are pretty convincing when they tell others about it. That approach appears to be part of making the whole tale a good story which will be believed by those who hear it. This last holdover from Berks County seems to accentuate this fact.

"Did you ever hear of the hoop snake?", asked the interesting herbalist, whose store was filled with strange-smelling dried herbs of all types. He had just brewed himself a cup of "Tansy" tea, and was now ready to regale us with the tales of long ago. "It had a horn on the end," he continued, "and it would roll, and whatever it hit when it opened up would die. My uncle swears he seen one go, and it hit a tree, and the tree died. I never could believe, but he says that positively he seen this. This was right up here."[2]

THE LOWER FORT

Battles of any kind always seem to generate many human interest stories, but the Indian wars here in Pennsylvania seem to have produced an exceptionally large number of these fascinating tales. Horrifying as some of them are, they do, on the other hand, preserve a picture of just how tough the people of those times had to be. Of all such records, there are probably none better than some of those about the Indian forts and blockhouses erected for protection of the settlers living on the Pennsylvania frontier. Most of these shelters are clearly mentioned in early county histories since names such as Fort Halifax, McClure's Fort, Bull Creek Blockhouse, and many others, were familiar places to the early settlers of the area where these "strong houses", as the Indians sometimes called them, were located. Havens of refuge from the fire brand and scalping knife, the fortresses were a necessary and permanent part of those early times when no one was sure whether they would wake up the next morning in heaven, amidst the fires of hell, or as a captive of Indian marauders.

As durable and secure as the forts were, it is not surprising that, even today, the memory of these old bastions still lives on in the names of the communities that eventually grew up around them. Examples of such places include Fort Louden in Franklin County, Forty Fort in Luzerne County, and Antes Fort in Lycoming County. However, in some cases more than just a name has survived. There are a few of the old stockades that are still in existence and which can be seen today. Fort McClure in Bloomsburg, Columbia County, and Rice's Fort in Milton, Union county, are two such examples. In Fayette County, Fort Gaddis remains as the only settlers' fort still

36

standing west of the Alleghenies. Nonetheless, the interest in the old forts has always been such that, even when the buildings no longer exist, people have sometimes decided to recreate them.

Replicas have been built of some forts like Fort Bedford, Bedford County, and Fort Necessity in Fayette County. Near Sunbury a one-sixth size scale model of Fort Augusta was once open to tourists. Here the fort's original well and powder magazine are still preserved, but in most cases historical markers are the sole reminders of the sites where the old stockades once stood. Fortunately, some of these places were commemorated just in time, before their significance and exact locations were lost forever.

One such fort which barely escaped oblivion existed in the eastern or "lower" end of Penns Valley, Centre County, near the village of Woodward. Known to early settlers as the "lower fort", it was one of three forts in the valley. Almost unmentioned in the history books, the lower fort was never forgotten by descendants of the settlers who once depended upon it for protection. Even today, there is an unusual legend about the bastion that was handed down from fathers to sons over the years, and which still surfaces now and then when the tales of olden times are retold in Penns Valley.

Besides the "lower fort" in the valley, there was an upper fort and a middle fort as well. Of the three forts, it has been the upper fort that has fared best in the history books. The reason for this is probably because the upper fort, also known as Potter's Fort, was the home of General James Potter, discoverer of the valley and veteran of the Revolutionary War and the French and Indian War. Unlike the upper fort, the other two valley forts never had a noted person like General Potter associated with them to help guarantee their place in history. Although General Potter mentions the lower fort in some of his letters, and alludes to a middle fort, the memory of both these stockades was kept alive mostly through folktales and legends, and it is the legend of the lower fort that takes us back to an age where all was not always romance and tranquility.

Fortunately, there have been descriptions preserved of the lower fort's appearance, which have been passed down to the present day. Once called the "Indian fort" rather than the lower fort, this settlers' refuge was about twenty to twenty-five feet long, eighteen feet wide, and seven to ten feet high. It was built of oak logs, shaped and fitted together very tightly. The settlers chose oak because oak trees were abundant in the area at that time, and because it is a particularly hard wood which does not ignite easily. Its hardness also made it an effective shield against bullets. As securely built as it was, there is little doubt that the building served as an effective place of defense against Indian war parties who would use any means at all to bring down a fortress like this one.

When attacking such forts, the Indians would often try to burn them down. In fact, one time when he must have been in a particularly cocky mood, Captain Jacobs, a noted Delaware war chief, bragged that he could "take any fort that will catch fire".[1] No accounts survive that say the Indians tried to burn the lower fort, but one record does say that "the early settlers had quite a contest with the Indians near the fort, which was on John Bowersox's place, and the graves of the killed were marked by quite a row of stones."[2]

Valley natives say that graves of some of these same settlers can still be seen today in Stover's Cemetery, just down the road from the site of the old stockade. "There's old settlers buried in that cemetery that were killed by Indians," claims one of the valley's native sons. "There was stones there, not regular stones like we have today, but it mentioned on there the man's name, and 'killed by Indians'.[3]

Tombstone inscriptions such as this may have been typical of the times when every man had to be a soldier. The epitaphs sound similar to another on a gravestone in an old burial ground in Lebanon County - another county where battles with Indians were common too. The closing line on the Lebanon County marker is "killed by the wilden". Wilden was a word the early German settlers here used to describe the Indians. It meant wild men.

Probably the man most knowledgeable about the settlers of the lower fort and their stories was Johnny Long. The valley farmer had lived on the site of the lower fort all his life, and he had heard tales from the old people who knew about the fort's legends. The enthralling stories must have captured the old man's imagination, for he managed to accumulate a large collection of Indian relics he found on his property over the years. Always willing to share his knowledge about the settlers' fort that once stood on his farm, Johnny Long did, however, keep one of his discoveries a secret until he was near the end of his life. Then, probably to insure that this last bit of unknown information about his beloved fort would not be forgotten, this son of sturdy pioneer stock revealed his secret to a life-long friend..

"He was older than I was," began Long's confidant. "When I started, he was up in the fifth or sixth grade already. He told me this here at Woodward Cave just a couple years before he died. He's sitting over there and talking and he said, 'Ray', - we got to talking about the Indians, you know, and about his fort. He said, 'Ray, I'm going to tell you something I never told anybody else. You and I were always good friends, from kids on up. You don't have to repeat it, but it's true or I wouldn't tell you.'

"He said, 'You remember a number of years ago, we built a new garage over there?' 'Well,' he said, 'Dad and I were digging a ditch to put in concrete to set the garage on. And as we dug this ditch,' he said, 'we dug up parts of a human body. The skull and legs and things like that, you know, but it was a human skull.' And he said, 'I don't know whether it was an Indian or whether it was a white man, you couldn't tell.'

"I asked him what he did with it," continued Long's old friend; "and he said, 'Well, it scared Dad. We dug it out and we throwed it in the concrete and poured concrete on it.'[3]

Even though he kept his gruesome discovery a secret for most of his life, this was not typical of Johnny Long when it came to telling everything else he knew about the old settlers' fort. Its history and legends seemed to be a continuing source of amusement for the old gentleman, and it was through him that some of the quaint details about the place have been saved. His recollections about the fort's cannons, for example, included the little-known fact that they had been strapped to logs and dragged there by horses. According to Mr. Long, the noise of these cannons did more to intimidate the Indian attackers than the cannon balls fired at them.

It seems also that the fort had been placed at the bottom rather than at the top of a hill, because at night the shapes of the marauding Indians coming over the hill could be more easily detected, outlined against the moon and stars, than they would have been if they were sneaking up to the fort from below. Unfortunately, many of Johnny Long's recollections about the fort were never documented, including anything he might have known about the man who was as closely identified with this fort as General Potter was with the upper fort - Jacob Stover, the man who couldn't be shot.

40

Jacob Stover and his brother, Adam, were among the first settlers in this part of Penns Valley, settling here in 1775. With exceptionally good farm land, due to its rich limestone soil, Penns Valley would later be settled, in part, by Revolutionary War veterans. They knew that here was one of the premier farming areas of the state, along with the lands of Buffalo Valley, Nittany Valley, and Lancaster County. The Stovers were, no doubt, attracted here for the same reason. The lower fort was built on Adam's land, with Round Head (*Rundkup*) Mountain to the east and Egg Hill (*Oie Holle*) to the west. So in the history books this place of defense should be recorded as Stover's Fort, if only to honor the memory of the family that was the driving force behind it.

Among the men whose families may have once sought shelter in the fort were six who had served with Northumberland County's rangers. These were men who had fought the Indians on the frontier. Some of these rangers had even been Indian captives, and one had almost starved before escaping. They were typical of many others who settled in eastern Penns Valley about the time of the Revolutionary War. Raw courage was considered to be one of the best qualities a man could have in those days, and, based on their war service, not one of these former rangers could ever have been charged with cowardice. However, it is Jacob Stover whose bravado seems to have been exceptional, since it is his story that lives on in the legends of the area.

Through the efforts of the late Dorothy Meyer, newspaper columnist and avid collector of the valley's legends, the following description of Jacob Stover has been preserved for posterity:
" He was big powerful blond man, who always wore a sword strapped around his waist and went without a shirt as soon as the seasons allowed. He wore his hair long, just like the Indians. He always treated the

Indians fairly and they had great respect for him and his sword. He was known as a man that could not be shot."[4]

Whether it was from the respect they held for him or because they were taken aback by his boldness, the Indians, so say the old legends, did not harm Jacob Stover, even when they could have ambushed him in the woods. What caused the Indians' unusual fear of this particular man is not documented, but people in those days, whites and Indians alike, were sometimes easily influenced by superstition and fear of the supernatural. Just how greatly signs and tokens could influence some Indians' actions and judgments in those days is revealed in an incident that happened after a massacre near the upper fort in 1778.

Express rider Robert Moore was probably enjoying a hint of spring in the air that day in May when he discovered the bodies of the Jacob Standford family on their farm, about three miles west of Potter's Fort. He entered the Standford homestead to say hello, but found the place to be strangely quiet. He then walked out and turned toward the spring that rises to the north of the cabin. Immediately he saw Mrs. Standford's body lying beside the pool of crystalline water that bubbles up from the cool depths of the earth. The unfortunate woman had been scalped a very short time before, as blood was yet seeping out of her wounds. Not too far away lay the bodies of her husband and their daughter. Moore alerted the garrison at Potter's, and a burial detail was despatched. The soldiers from the fort soon had the victims' bodies interred "in a corner of one of the fields".[5]

Sometime after this, several of Robert Moore's horses wandered off into the Seven Mountains, and he went looking for them. Perhaps the express rider's Indian instincts, for he was the adopted son of an Indian chief, made his senses particularly acute that day, or perhaps it was just luck, but whatever the case, he made another grisly discovery. Near a large pine log he noticed a pile of leaves, which aroused his curiosity. Upon closer inspection, he uncovered the well-preserved body of an Indian. The man had evidently been killed upon the spot, and it appeared he had been quickly abandoned, for lying with him were all his accoutrements and his rifle.

Some years later, when the whites and the Indians were at peace, Mr. Moore met an aged Indian chief called Captain Hunt. The old warrior claimed he had been with the party of Indians who had massacred the Standfords. He also explained that, after they had murdered the Standfords, they decided they would also raid settlers over the Seven Mountains in Kishacoquillas Valley, present-day Mifflin County. They set off on their dastardly mission, traveling in an easterly direction.

Soon they arrived at the gap which led over the mountains to the valley where Chief Logan lived beside his famous spring. Then a detonation ripped the air, and one of their chiefs lay dead. Unexplicably, his gun had exploded and the blast killed him on the spot. This remarkable event so intimidated the Indians that they concluded the occurrence was an "ill omen". Whereupon, they called a council, and it was agreed that their raid into the Kishacoquillas Valley should be abandoned. They then quickly fled the area, but not before they covered their leader "hastily with leaves."[6]

Beliefs and actions of the white settlers in those times were just as apt to be influenced by superstitious fears. Some of the things that were thought to be possible then seem outrageous to us today. Examples of such types of beliefs, which were, no doubt, common during Jacob Stover's lifetime, were once prevalent in many parts of the state.

In Schuylkill County, for example, the notion once existed that the earliest settlers there "had books by which they could render themselves invisible to pursuing Indians or change themselves into logs."[7] In fact, in that same county a story was once told about a man there who changed himself into a log to hide from Indians who were chasing him. The legend claims that "so many Indians came and sat on the log that he could scarcely bear the weight of them."[7]

Actually, stories about men changing themselves into logs could have been based on real events. With a little embellishment on the part of the storyteller, an actual, similar, incident might have ended up as an exaggerated story like the Schuylkill County tale. One event that just might have been the basis for stories about men changing themselves into logs to escape Indian pursuers is recorded in a history of the Wyoming Valley, Wyoming County. Settlers here were regularly attacked by Indians, and after one such invasion, in 1763, people fled the area in droves.

The Indians pursued the runaways unmercifully, and it was said the fugitives endured such hardship that "no pen can describe their suffering".[8] Among those fleeing for their lives was a man named Noah Hopkins. Quicker than most, Hopkins was able to distance himself from his pursuers, but he must have realized that sooner or later his stamina would be no match for the Indians. All at once he spotted the huge trunk of a fallen forest monarch. Noting that the log was hollow, Hopkins quickly slipped into it. Here he lay, absolutely still, for several hours.

Just as he was probably starting to feel that he had finally eluded his pursuers, Hopkins could hear their footsteps. With their moccasined feet pounding the forest path as they ran, the determined Indians remained doggedly on their quarry's trail. Shortly afterwards, the terrified frontiersman heard three of the Indian braves sit down on the very log in which he was hiding. They began to discuss what their next move should be, and Hopkins would later recall that they were so close he could hear the rattling sound of the bullets in their bullet pouches.

Shortly after, one of the braves got off the log and looked into one end. He could not see the silent frontiersman lying as still as a dead man. Years later Hopkins would say that the Indians failed to discover him because "a spider had woven a web over the entrance shortly after he entered the hollow log."[9] The Indians eventually went on their way, but Hopkins stayed in the log as long as he could stand it. Then, after he was almost starved, he cautiously crawled out, and fought his way through the thick forests until he was safely back at a white settlement.

So Noah Hopkins story, if not an exaggerated account itself, could certainly have been the source for legends about men turning themselves into logs to escape Indians. Similarly, the legend that no one could shoot Jacob Stover may have been an embellished account that attempted to explain why the Indians never bothered him. His fellow settlers probably thought his life was a charmed one. They may have attempted to rationalize his immunity by presuming that he was endowed with the power of invincibility.

FOOTNOTE:

The Jacob Standford cabin still stands along Rimmey Road in Potter Township, Centre County. The outside has been restored to the way it looked when the Standfords lived there, and the little spring which supplied the Standfords with liquid refreshment still flows as it did during the day when its waters may have been dyed red with the blood of valley pioneers. The graves of the Standfords were forgotten over time, and, despite heroic efforts by men like J. Marvin Lee, and other valley historians. they remain lost to this day.

The lower fort did not fare as well as the Standford cabin. Sometime late in the last century or in the early years of this one, the old fortress was demolished, and now only its legends remain. What a thrill it would be today to stand upon the same floorboards those early valley settlers once stood upon while defending themselves from the stalwart sons of the forest - under the same roof, in fact, that sheltered Adam Stover himself.

Site of the Lower Fort (top)

& The Standford Cabin (bottom)

Centre County

SPELL-BOUND

Some of the old-time stories about witches and witchcraft sound pretty fantastic to us today, but we have to keep in mind that these were tales based upon generations of popular folk beliefs. Although they were completely unscientific, these notions about the supernatural things that witches could do are really a record of how our ancestors tried to find reasons behind events that were, to them, unexplainable. We shouldn't think that they were silly or ignorant because of the way they thought; they were merely uninformed, mainly because they didn't have the educational opportunities that would have taught them to think differently and discard centuries-old ideas. This is the situation that should be kept in mind, then, when we read of the supernatural things that people once believed were within witches' powers to perform. And certainly ranking up there with some of the most fantastic of these notions would have to be the belief that a witch could render people or animals immobile by just using a magical incantation or some other sinister procedure. There was even a name for beasts or persons who had been placed in such states; they were said to be "fastened" or "spell-bound".

Tales of induced immobility were once common throughout the Keystone State, but they seemed especially prevalent wherever you would find limestone soil. At first this seems silly, but there used to be a belief here claiming that if you were standing on Pennsylvania limestone soil and started speaking Pennsylvania Dutch, you would "get a response every time".[1] This belief was based on the fact that the Pennsylvania Dutch were prone to follow "the trail of limestone soil and the walnut tree"[2] because this was the best farming country for growing crops. Consequently, it's not surprising that one way to find the origins of some of the oldest legends and folktales in Pennsylvania, including the stories about witches rendering animals and people immobile, is to follow the same trail the Pennsylvania Dutchman once followed, starting over in the Blue Mountains of Berks and Lebanon Counties.

Witch stories certainly were very popular subjects when storytellers would spin their yarns around the cracker barrels of country stores in any part of Pennsylvania's "Dutch" country, but most of these tales have been long forgotten. However, due to dedicated efforts by some early collectors, a number of quaint tales from the Blue Mountains of Berks and Lehigh Counties were saved for all time. Among these are some typical episodes about witches causing horses to freeze in their tracks.

Over near the village of Orefield, Lehigh County, there was a widely circulated tale a number of years ago about a teamster who had a fine set of horses to drag his logs. The team could pull almost any load, except when they came to the same level stretch of ground near a house which sat alongside an old country road. Here the horses would stop dead in their tracks and refuse to move any further, as though held in place by some mysterious force. The first time it happened, the teamster noticed a man working on the roof of the house. The second time it happened, the teamster saw the same man on the roof, and, realizing the man had spell-bound his horses, commanded him to "stop your nonsense". Then when it happened a third time, the disgusted teamster took his knife, stuck it into the horse collar of his saddle horse, and shouted to the man on the roof, "I'll teach you a lesson." At that same time the roofer, so says the tale, "fell down dead".[3]

Many similar tales were once told in the Blue Mountains of Berks, Lehigh, and Lebanon Counties, and all had the same basic outlines: a man's horses refused to move or pull as a result of being "fastened", and their exasperated owner resorts to some violent act to remedy the situation. In addition to sticking a knife into a horse's collar, a person might also shoot a bullet into his wagon's wheel, or take an ax and knock some spokes out of the wheel. According to the old tales, the result of such actions was that the person doing the hexing would fall over dead or immediately come forth begging for mercy lest they die.

There was once a popular tale like this over in Centre County, near the small village of Spring Mills. "It was bewitching," claimed the old mountain man, who was born in 1885, and who claimed he saw such things more than once. "I know my dad's team was [bewitched] a good many times," the man continued. "Yeah, they wouldn't pull the cap off your head. Once me and pop [Aaron Auman] went over in Little Poe Valley picking huckleberries. A young guy from Greenbrier was there, and Eunie Lingle and his son were hauling rye. They had poor horses. They were poor people in Poe Valley, you know. They were coming around the barn. I said, 'Oh, look over there - that big load of rye is going around the barn.' This young guy said, 'Let's have some fun,' and he took a string out of his pocket and pulled a knot in it, and, do you know, they couldn't start those horses. They couldn't get those horses to move. What you see with your own eyes, you have to believe. The old man, he started to howl, and I said, 'You ought to be shot! Those poor horses. That's the Devil's work."[4]

Accounts like this made good stories to tell one's neighbors, and such tales enjoyed a wide circulation. A few of them also managed to survive to the present day, along with some of the hard feelings that were sometimes created when the accounts tarnished the reputation of a relative. When the preceding episode appeared in print some seventy years after the event occurred, Eunie Lingle's descendant could still get upset over the implications.

"I had a notion once to arrest them," declared Lingle's grandson in 1988, taking exception to the statement that Eunie Lingle kept "poor horses". "That was runnin' my grandpa down, you know," explained the grandson, "and I guess Aaron Auman was the one that done it. That's the kind of things he did. He must've been a pow-wower if he took those horses' strength away. When he was die'n', I heard say that he said, 'The Devil's comin' down along the wall with a pitchfork to get me!'"[5]

Such stories must have convinced a number of people that witches actually could freeze horses in their tracks. Notions like this seem far-fetched to us today, but what seems even more surprising is that those who should have had adequate "horse sense" didn't apply that knowledge to come up with logical explanations for their horses' refusal to move. One Berks County man, who had grown up handling his grandfather's horses, thought that the animals were just defiant at times.

"I know my grandfather's horse was the stubborn kind," offered the decidedly "Dutch", Pennsylvania Dutchman. "We had a load of hay loaded and all of a sudden he stopped and he wouldn't move. My Grandfather was on the wagon trying to get him to go, and I was down; and I got a hold of him and I got mad and I hit him on the head and knocked him out. I didn't know if you hit a horse a certain place it knocks him out. I didn't know that, and my grandfather said, 'You killed the horse! You killed it!' I never forgot that. After a while [the horse] got up again, and then he could go."[6]

Even more fantastic than the old-time belief that witches could render horses immobile was the idea that they could also "fasten" people. Once again, there seems to have been very little attempt, sometimes, to find logical explanations when some poor person was in the throes of a seizure or similar malady. Then, too, witch stories were good entertainment, and any tale about a witch freezing a person in his or her tracks was, no doubt, highly embellished as it was told and retold. However, based on the tales like this that I was able to find, it would appear that the more recent the chronicle the less colorful it sometimes seems to be. Perhaps this is an indication that people became less likely to believe in such things as they became more educated. Readers can judge this for themselves as they digest the episodes that follow, and which are arranged from the youngest to the oldest. All supposedly occurred within the last one-hundred and fifty years, and all deal with someone who was spell-bound.

The first account occurred about twenty-five years ago in Potter Township, of Centre County. Here, near the small village of Locust Grove, an incident occurred around "butchering time", which was traditionally done in the fall of the year.

"We butchered here one year," recalled the valley farmer, "and Lila I. and Catherine P. got into a round when the butcherin' was done. So Catherine and them went home first. It couldn't have been more than an hour or so after they went home, why, Bob [Catherine's husband] called up and he said, 'There's somethin' the matter with Kate. She's layin' down here on the bed and can't move. Can you come down?'

"So I went down, and sure as hen, there she was, stretched out like a poker. And he said, 'What'da ya think I ought'a do?'

"Well," I said, "the only thing I know is to take her to the doctor." Cause I didn't know, you know, if she might'a twisted herself or what. And I wasn't home here long until the telephone rang. Here it was Lila.

"She said, 'Did you get a telephone call?

"I said, 'Yeah. Somethin' happened to Kate."

"She said, 'You go down?'

"I said, 'Yeah.'

"She said, 'Well, you shouldn't't've!" [This statement, according to the narrator, meant that his visit broke the spell].

Well, I didn't know what the hen was goin' on, you know. Bob, he took her up to the doctor, at the hospital dispensary. They checked her over and couldn't find nothin'. They helped her off'a the litter up there, and then she come home, and that was the end of it."[7]

This next account is also from Centre County, where a man and his girl friend got into an argument some fifty or sixty years ago, and the man used his occult powers to teach her a lesson - at least that's what some folks claimed.

"Did you know that Charlie S. that stayed out here with Pearl D.?," asked the man who was quite an authority on the witch tales of Penns Valley. "He was another character. He stayed with that Pearl, and he had that house down there that they used for a summer home. They went down there one day, and he said, 'Are you goin' along Pearl?'

'No.', she said. 'You fool around too much when you go down there.'

'No,' he said. 'We ain't gonn'a be down there long today.'

"So she went along, and, of course, old Charles started workin' around, you know, and Pearl started moanin' about goin' home. And old Charles said, 'Now don't get in a hurry. We'll leave after bit.'

'If you don't soon get ready,' she said, 'I'm just gonn'a walk home.'

'No,' he said, 'you ain't walkin' home.' She said, 'I'll show you'.

"So old Charles, he kept workin' around there, and Pearl, she got on him again about takin' 'em home.

"Charles said, 'I told you, you'll go when I'm ready', and she said, 'I'm walkin'!'

He said, 'No you ain't!'

"And she started for the door, and when she grabbed the door and went to sling it open, just as she got in the doorway, that's all the further she went. Boy she stood there, they said, and she squealed and hollered and went on."[7]

This wasn't the only story of this type that local authorities on such matters had heard. Another man from the same valley recalled that a friend of his had once told him that a witch had entered his bedroom one night and had thrown a cover over him as he slept. "And he said, 'I couldn't talk; I couldn't holler; I couldn't speak; I couldn't do nothin'. There I laid!'[5]

Such tales were not unique to Centre County, as Sam Bayard found out when he was collecting folk tunes in Greene County about sixty-five years ago. The place where the incident occurred was near the villages of Deep Valley and New Freeport, Greene County.

"This Mrs. Rodgers, told me," recalled Bayard, "that when she was a girl, her whole family was paralyzed one time in their beds when a group of people entered the house. The door was supposed to be locked, but they came right in. Mrs. Rodgers' mother had her little short pipe laid up on the chest of drawers beside the bed, and some one of these guys took it down and smoked it a while, and then laid it aside. They couldn't move out of their beds while these people were poking around there, and then they left.

"I said, 'Well, who was them people?', and she said, 'Witches!' They were not able to make a move until the people had left the house!"[8]

This next tale is probably well over one-hundred years old, because the lady who told me the story was born in 1905, and she had heard the story from her grandmother, who claimed she experienced the encounter with the black cat first-hand. It's an interesting account - one that you could even call spell-binding, because it brings in the notion that black cats and witches are sometimes one and the same thing. This old belief was preserved in a once-popular saying here in Pennsylvania - a proverb that claimed, 'When a witch disappears a black cat appears.'[9]

"I heard my grandmother tellin', " began the venerable old Centre County lady, "that right out the road there, [south of the mountain called Egg Hill, in Georges Valley, Centre County], she went down to the barn. She was gonn'a feed - put hay in, you know; feedin' whatever she was feedin'. And, of course, here set a great black cat, and the cat wouldn't move. So she kicked at it, and when she kicked at it, why she couldn't move. She just stood there - had to stand there. All at once, then, the cat disappeared, and then she could move. She could walk, you know, to get away from where she was standing."[10]

This was not an unusual story for the period in which it was set. Common ideas about witchcraft, even down to middle of the twentieth century, included the belief that witches could turn into cats or almost anything else in order to get at their quarry. For example, one such idea included the notion that a witch "could turn herself into a fly, and crawl through a keyhole."[11] Another tenct was that witches would "work" on people through an animal that couldn't control itself. "I seen this," claimed one believer. "In fact, they say the reason this one woman had all these cats [was] because she worked through them cats onto people. It's weird!"[12]

Most people today would agree that such tales are "weird", and don't give them a second thought. Certainly, we know now that spell-binding only makes for good stories, and is not something that a professed witch can do to animals or to other people. However, there also used to be a belief that a person could, by "fastening", easily apprehend a thief who had robbed them. Merely through reciting a whole series of sentences containing many references to Christ and the Almighty, the robbery victim could, it was believed, immobilize a criminal when these last sentences of the invocation were spoken:

Ye thieves, I bind you with the same bonds with what Jesus our Lord has bound hell; and thus ye shall be bound.
In the name of the Father, the Son, and the Holy Ghost;
and the same words that bind you shall also release you.[13]

Undoubtedly, most of us look upon such conjuring as quaint reminders of our dim past. On the other hand, given today's crime rate at times, there are probably just as many of us who might think that the ability to spell-bind thieves would be a nice weapon to have in our arsenal against the evils of the present age.

LAST OF THE BIG SHOTS

Throughout the United States there are numerous folk tales dealing with great hunters and their remarkable prowess with fantastic rifles. Such stories range from the one about Paul Bunyan and his big gun having twenty-six barrels, to the ingenious hunter who loaded his musket with nails, so that when he shot an animal it was nailed to a tree. In fact, it would seem that the variations on such themes are limited only by the imaginations of the storytellers who enjoy telling these "whoppers" to anyone who can be duped into believing the story being told is true - right up until the time the last sentence is delivered.

It is from this type of good-natured lying that so many tales like this have been concocted; and it is because they are so humorous that they've lasted so long. Who cannot enjoy tales about the hunter whose telescopic sight was so powerful that it brought a distant group of pigs up so close that he could hear their squeals and grunts? Just as funny is the one about the hunter whose gun shoots so far that by the time he gets to the game he's killed, the meat has spoiled. Of course, another common tall-tale along the same lines is the one about the hunter who kills many animals with a single shot. Typical of this type is the story about the marksman who sees a huge flock of birds one day. He takes aim with the great gun he's carrying, and fires one shot. Immediately, many mortally-wounded birds start dropping from the sky at such a rate that they soon bury the hunter with their bodies.

Hunters here in Pennsylvania probably have heard many of these exaggerated stories, including the one from Potter County about the hunter who stumbles upon a flock of pigeons in a farmer's field.

58

Each bird in the flock is sitting on a stake in the ground, and the stakes form a circle around a haystack in the middle of the field. Determined to kill as many birds as he can with one shot, the hunter lays his rifle barrel over a boulder and bends it into a curve. He then aims, so that the curved gun barrel coincides with the circle of stakes, fires, and kills all the pigeons but one.

Probably one of the most widespread Pennsylvania tall tales dealing with fantastic shooting has to do with the farmer who hears a lot of noise in his chicken coop one night. This story has surfaced in Tioga County, but it has also been heard in other parts of the state as well. In Centre County the episode circulated around the State College area for many years, finding a particular fondness for the farms near the villages of Houserville and Lemont.

"Bill Everhart was a farmer that lived up on the Branch Road", recalled one valley native, "and here he raised a bunch of chickens. He had prized hens. They were good layers. One night Bill went to bed; it was in the fall of the year. It was pretty cold and Bill was wearing long underwear already. He went to bed that night, and during the night he heard these hens making an awful fuss.

"Bill decided there was a fox or something after the hens, so he slipped on his shoes and coat and hat, and grabbed his shotgun and flashlight, and went out to the chicken coop. He didn't have any pants on, but he had those longjohns on with the 'barn door' in the back. He walked up to the door and he opened the door, and was standing there holding the light and shining into the chicken coop, and held the gun ready, you know. And his dog came up and put his cold nose against his rear end and scared Bill. His gun went off and he shot twenty of his good hens."[1]

Bill Everhart was still living at the time the story with his name in it was told to me, and so, in order to verify the authenticity of the anecdote, I called the old farmer and asked him if he knew he was the "hero" of this oft-repeated account. The lifelong valley husbandman accepted the question good-naturedly, noting, "Harry Resides started that story and put my name in it. Harry used to run a taxi service in State College. I never appreciated that he put my name in it. I guess he thought it was a good joke. In the first place I'd never be dumb enough to go out to the chicken house in my underwear at night. I heard it was Walter Bickel that that happened to, but he probably won't admit it."[2]

At this point I realized that any man who had accidentally shot that many of his own chickens was probably not about to confess it. On the other hand, maybe, if enough years had passed, he would be able to look back on the episode with a sense of humor. In any case, I knew I was not likely to find the person to be a braggart like Pittsburgh's Mike Fink, the notorious raftsman of the Ohio and Mississippi Rivers. Fink, it was said, once boasted that he could "out-run, out-jump, out-shoot, out-brag, out-drink, an' out-fight, rough-an'-tumble, no holds barred, ary man on both sides the river from Pittsburgh to New Orleans".[3]

Hoping that I wouldn't have to travel as far as Pittsburgh while following the trail of my infamous chicken killer, I contacted Walter Bickel. Although not exactly finding the culprit I was after, I think I did finally discover how this particular legend found a home in State College. After I had related the story to Bickel, he replied, "No, that didn't happen to me. I've heard that story though. I think that was just a joke. Maybe it did happen somewhere. My dad, Alonzo, was a poor shot. He was the kind that was not safe to have a gun. I thought after my mother died I'd get him to go out hunting with me. He had one of them hammer guns - a double-barreled gun with hammers on. And when he'd pull a hammer back he wouldn't get his finger off the trigger, and off she'd go, right down at his feet. I thought that was enough of that. I wouldn't take him hunting anymore."[4]

There were, however, two other episodes that Walter Bickel remembered about his father's mishandling of a gun that began to sound more and more like the legend of the farmer who accidentally shot his chickens one night. Bickel recalled both tales with a sense of humor.

"One night there was somebody in the chicken house, and he went stumpin' out to the chicken house, and got some clay in the gun, in the barrel. He didn't know it was in there, and the next day he went out to shoot at a crow. Used to be a lot of crows in the corn field in the spring, pullin' the corn. He went out and shot at the crow, and the gun flew all apart - blew up because there was mud in the barrel. All he had was the stock in his hand. The barrel flew off. He was so miserable with a gun anyway. He didn't know how to handle a gun.

"Another night he heard a noise out there, so he shot towards the chicken house, with fine shot. He shot through the porch post; put a hole right through it. It was just made out of boards - boards about a foot wide, four boards. So he blowed a hole right through there, off the porch towards the chicken house."[4]

Based on Bill Everhart's comments and Walter Bickel's recollections, it's obviously safe to say that the story of the farmer's accidental shooting of his own chickens is a popular legend that may have arisen from a real life incident which some imaginative storyteller embellished in order to make the story more humorous. Once it was created, however, it took on a life of its own. Like all legends, it now migrates from place to place; and in all cases it is adopted as that locale's own story. It appears that it gets associated with someone who's already got a reputation as a poor handler of firearms. The entry of the legend into the State College area, for example, was probably made that much easier because of Alonzo Bickel's many mishaps with guns.

HAUNTS OF THE HIGHWAY

Stories of people vanishing into thin air seem far-fetched to those of us who would actually have to see this happen before we'd believe it, but tales of such things have been around a long time. In fact, in the legendary realm there is one particular anecdote that has made the rounds for at least a hundred years in this country, and probably even longer if some serious study was done on the matter. However, the problem confronting interested students of such things is that any research is difficult due to the elusive qualities of the material.

In the first place, supernatural phenomena do not lend themselves to methodical study. They are not repeatable upon request, nor are they controllable. They are somewhat like oil droplets floating in the waters of scientific inquiry in that they doggedly remain separate from our earthly realm. Even when such events do manifest themselves, they still manage to remain as unworldly as they ever were, leading scientists to dismiss them as unworthy of further study of any kind. In fact, despite the possibility that such events could represent some manifestation of a real natural phenomenon we just don't understand yet, the modern day attitude toward ghosts and related events still often seems to be that only foolish folks believe in such things anymore.

Maybe it is the fear of being ridiculed that leads those who think they've seen a ghost to remain silent about it. On the other hand, since people today are less likely than their great grandparents to believe in such things, they do not find stories of "spooks" or of haunted houses over on the mountain worth repeating. The modern day view is that ghosts just do not exist; they are the product of overactive imaginations or of tired minds. But this is an attitude that clashes with that of fifty or sixty years ago when belief in such things was still fairly strong compared to the view we enlightened types take toward these matters today. However, there is good reason for scepticism about these tales, for they do acquire legendary qualities, circulating blithely from mountain to mountain and often settling down where they seem most comfortable.

The persistent episode which was mentioned in the first paragraph is a perfect example of this type of situation. It is an anecdote which has circulated in this country for decades, and it has most certainly found several homes here in Pennsylvania. Popularly known as "The Vanishing Hitchhiker", one variant of the story appears to have settled in Fulton County at an earlier time and in the area of that county known as "The Lockins", so-named for the way Tuscarora Mountain and Scrub Ridge seemingly lock together, forming one of the wildest and most remote spots in that section of Penn's Woods. The yarn itself appears to have been popular here around the turn of the century, and since its details come from unreliable sources, I don't wish to elaborate upon it any further, other than just noting that the tale apparently was once found in this part of the state.

Decades ago such accounts were easy to find all over the Keystone State, and today the uninterested or uninformed might get the impression that local ghost stories are rarely talked about at all any more; that every ghost has been put to rest, or "laid", as the old-timers used to say. However, restless spirits are not quieted that easily, and, if one can believe the local tales that still surface now and again, the same ghosts frequent much the same places they did when "grandpap" saw them fifty years ago. Taking this a step further, it might be stated that if enough people around present-day McConnelsburg , Fulton County, were interviewed, one of them could probably tell the interested listener a vanishing hitchhiker anecdote that is similar to the same Tuscarora Mountain story that was popular here around the turn of the century. Moreover, in all probability the episode would be related as having actually happened recently, rather than being recounted as just some sort of ancient fairy tale.

Similarly, some folks living in Luzerne and Lackawanna Counties can relate their own rendition of the same yarn, and this one, too, they say, was an actual event, occurring within the last twenty years. The setting for this version of the legend is quite typical since the account of the vanishing hitchhiker is always said to occur at some remote spot in the mountains. In this case the mountains are those wild and rugged ridges called the Moosic Mountains.

During the early days when enormous herds of elk ranged through the Lackawanna Valley and over the Appalachian ridges around it, the Indians apparently found this to be a fine place to hunt. In fact, so successful were they in finding elk on these lands that they named the spot *Moosic*, or "Elk Place"[1] Today there are no reminders of the great elk herds which were exterminated by the whites, nor are there many artifacts left of the original Indian inhabitants of the region. Once the white settlers became masters of the valley, it did not take long for them to alter it to suit themselves. Within the span of several centuries, the once-verdant region, which had taken millions of years to perfect, was converted to a product of the industrial era, with railroads, slag heaps, and strip mines becoming some of its most dominant features.

Despite this short-sighted assault on the "great meadows" of the Lenni Lenape, the ageless mountains remained in an untamed state, displaying all the splendor and evoking as much inspiration as they did before whites even entered the valley. Even today, anyone driving over the Moosics cannot escape their magnificence nor fail to be impressed by the picturesque views of the countryside below. However, the cool pine forest on either side of the roadway conveys a feeling of loneliness to the solitary traveler, and the density of the forest also lends a dark and somber air to the surroundings. Nonetheless, despite this single melancholy touch, there is solitude here, and from these tranquil heights even the placid valleys below seem to have escaped the ravages of progress and the vagaries of time.

Time means a lot to some people, and to others it's not all that important, but in the ghostly realm time means nothing at all. Here sun dials and hour glasses are for mere mortals, and the passing of seconds, minutes, and hours is simply a concept devised in the minds of men. At least that's probably the rationale that's behind the story of the odd hitchhiker that was picked up by a local school teacher as he was driving through the Moosic Mountains one rainy night. The weather was, in fact, just ideal for the encounter that is described in this legend that once was widely circulated throughout the Lackawanna Valley.

"Mister R. was a teacher in the Pittston School District," began the Pittston native who had heard this tale from his mother. "He was a Korean War vet who had both legs taken off. One fall night he was driving from Pittston to Scranton on the Scranton/Wilkes-Barre Highway. At a place called Duryea, near the Avoca Airport, he spotted a hitchhiker close to Kay's Restaurant. He was a clean-cut kid about eighteen years old. The boy told him where he was going, and being it was a rainy night, Mr R. stopped and agreed to give him a ride. Mr. R. had his wheel chair and some books in the front seat, so the kid got into the back. They did talk, but when Mr R. got to Scranton, he looked in the back seat and the boy was gone! He never stopped or slowed down enough for the boy to get out.

"After taking care of his business in Scranton, Mr. R. remembered the address the boy gave him, so he went to the house. A woman answered, and he told her what happened. The woman told him that it was her son, who was killed four years prior to this in the very spot that he picked him up. He described him to the letter, and it fit perfect to a description of the kid. The woman said that this had happened three times before - different people had picked him up."[2]

Women are featured in the accounts of the vanishing hitchhiker in other ways as well. Consider a tale of frustrated lovers that was once popular in Blair County. The setting for the narrative is near the famous railroad landmark known as the Horseshoe Curve, which is located on that part of the Allegheny front known locally as "Wopsy" Mountain. On top of this ridge, which rises to a height of 2600 feet, can be found the Wopsononock Tableland. The view from here is one of the finest in the state, affording a fantastic view of Altoona and of seemingly endless mountains that span six counties. It is a beautiful spot - too beautiful for the legend that has settled on this same mountain.

The legend of Wopsy Mountain's Woman in White was related to me by a resident of Altoona, the town that is appropriately nick-named "the Mountain City" because of the magnificent peaks that surround it. This lively lady of eighty years was fully convinced that the legend of the lady in white and her forbidden lover is a true story.

"They wanted to get married, and her daddy wouldn't let her marry him," recalled the spunky octogenarian. "They lived in a great big mansion somewhere up on Wopsy Mountain, and she was gonna' marry him anyhow. So she was gonna' run away with him.

"Well, they got in this carriage, and when they got down to where the curve goes like this, the wagon runs off the road and his head was cut off. She couldn't find him, and she hunted everywhere. Now she comes down the mountain; not every day, mostly around evening 'cause you can see her white dress. She's huntin' for his head.

"One rainy day a man was coming down, and she was standing by the road. It was just gettin' dark, and he stopped and asked her if she wanted a ride. Well, she got in the car, and when he got into Altoona she wasn't there. But the seat was wet where she was sitting, so he knew that he had picked her up. And he said he don't know when she got out or how she got out, because he didn't hear the car door. They always called her the 'woman in white'.

"My son went up, and he set up there nearly all night. He was gonna' watch for her. And he told the guys, he says, 'I'm going home. She ain't gonna come anyhow.' So he turned around and come home."[3]

One common thing about these narratives, other than their basic content, is that the person who tells them believes they are relating the details of an actual event. In other words, the narrator doesn't adopt this narrative style just to enhance the listener's enjoyment or to try to fool anyone. Many people actually believe that such things did, and do, occur. What's more probable, however, is that this story is such good entertainment that it gets widely circulated. After all, if victims of automobile crashes often came back as ghostly hitchhikers there would be a lot of them along route 322 in the Lewistown Narrows between Lewistown and Arch Rock, Mifflin County. Locals here have placed small white crosses along the roadside to commemorate victims of car accidents that have claimed so many lives. On the south side of the highway the Juniata River flows calmly along until it joins the mighty Susquehanna River at Clarks Ferry, Dauphin County. Remains of the Pennsylvania Canal, built in 1826, can still be seen on this same side of the highway, but on the other side are the crosses - there were forty-eight in October, 1996. There is also (October, 1996), the sign: "You must go through Death Valley to get to Happy Valley".

Travelers going to "Happy Valley", the name students have given to State College and the Penn State campus there, will do well to drive carefully through this narrow defile of 2000 foot high Shade Mountain. If the name of the mountain is not warning enough (spirits of the departed were once called "shades" in the old days), then the crosses should be. They at least should remind drivers of the hazardous driving conditions here, and can also bring to mind the tales of ghostly hitchhikers that were supposedly created by car accidents in places just like this.

MORE SNAKES

Various quaint notions and superstitions about snakes have arisen over the centuries, and most of these beliefs are not very complimentary. These unfavorable views probably arose in part due to peoples' ignorance about snakes and their habits. The Bible, of course, with its story of Adam and Eve and the serpent in the Garden of Eden, did absolutely nothing for snakes' public relations. In fact, it is probably the unfavorable light that is cast upon them in the Bible that caused people over the centuries to steadfastly believe that vipers were associated with the supernatural and with the powers of darkness.

Examples of these uncomplimentary beliefs include the one that snakes can hypnotize their prey. This idea, of course, probably made a superstitious person even more fearful when they disturbed a sleeping black snake lying in the grass, and it rose up in front of them like a cobra - which black snakes will do. The belief about hypnotism perhaps arose from the fact that snakes have no visible eyelids, and so their eyes never appear to close, and from the fact that snakes have very poor eyesight. Since their vision is so poor, snakes must watch a moving object very carefully, as if trying to hypnotize it, in order to determine if that object is something that could serve as their next meal.

Another widely-held misconception about vipers is the idea that a mortally wounded snake won't die until sundown. Such a belief probably once again arose from the Biblically-based superstition that snakes have infernal powers and are in league with the devil. The fact is, snakes are cold-blooded. This means that right after one is killed, its muscles, warmed by the sun, will continue to twitch until sundown, after which the snake's body will cool down and muscle spasms will cease.

Given all these weird notions about snakes, it's no wonder that people developed the idea that vipers are things to be feared and to be avoided. Consequently, various superstitions also arose about what things were effective in warding off serpents of all kinds. Branches from either ash trees or hazel bushes were thought to be particularly good repellents, and fern leaves were said to be a good material for making a bed in the woods since their smell would also supposedly chase away poisonous animals.

Since snakes were so numerous a century or more ago, both in the woods and around peoples' homes, folks then probably tended to be more wary of these reptiles. Some of the intense fear that people must have harbored against snakes seems to be exemplified in at least two categories of stories. The first preserves a superstition that people had about what snakes could do to children. The second seems to reveal what peoples' thoughts used to be concerning how supernatural forces could use snakes as weapons against mankind.

The old belief about what effects snakes could have on children was once prevalent in Greene County and in neighboring Fayette County, where there was "the story about the child who fed the snake, and whose mother interfered, whereupon the child pined away and died. My own mother told me about that. She had often heard it."[1]

In the central part of the state, around State College, there was also once a popular tale similar to the Fayette County anecdote. Here a Pennsylvania "Dutchman" named Jacob Houser is accorded the honor of being the first white settler in what is now College Township, Centre County. The year was 1788, and the vast virgin forest land that would become the site of one of the most highly-respected universities in the country was, literally, a howling wilderness. However, the primeval conditions of the area didn't stop the little German immigrant from taming it, and eventually he built a small log cabin along the stream now called Spring Creek.

Houser was just twenty-eight at the time, and in his prime, toughened by his service with the Lancaster County militia in the Revolutionary War. His naturally high energy levels, and the fact that he was descended from sturdy Dauphin County pioneer "stock", filled him with a driving ambition to succeed. Evidence of his efforts began to appear around his homestead in the form of a grist mill, a saw mill, and eventually a fulling mill with a carding machine. His land holdings and his family began to grow in proportion to his other successes, and soon Houser had a son and heir.

The Houser cabin was too small to hold a large family, which eventually would grow to three sons and five daughters, and so the Housers soon talked about building a bigger place. Then during the heavy spring rains of 1800, the swollen waters of Spring Creek flooded the Houser cabin, and that decided the issue. Eventually a larger place was erected higher up on the hill, and it was at this new homestead that some rather astounding events occurred - at least that's what is claimed in a Houser family tradition that has come down to us in the form of a legend. Origins of this story will prove surprising to those who don't realize how ancient the roots of tales like this can be.

Time has erased all evidence of Jacob Houser's original pioneer buildings, except for traces of his old millrace along Spring Creek. However, the memory of this Centre County pioneer is perpetuated in the name of the village that grew up on the site of his industrial complex and homestead - the town of Houserville. In addition to this singular honor, there is also a memory of the family preserved in the aforementioned legend that has been handed down through generations of the Houser family - a legend about Jacob's first son, Martin, and a snake that visited the new cabin on the hill.

According to the family traditions, the Housers planted a sizeable garden beside the new homestead. The fresh vegetables that would grow here would provide a welcome supplement to an otherwise plain diet, and so, like most pioneer families of that day, the Housers tended the plot with care. The cultivated strip of land, with its neat and even rows of plants, must have been attractive to a five year old boy, for one hot summer day Martin wandered into the garden carrying a tin cup his mother had filled with a snack of cool milk and fresh pieces of bread. Here Martin decided to sit down and savor his little treat, content to just enjoy peaceful country breezes and to dream of the things that fill little boys' heads with wonder.

Mrs. Houser forgot about her son's whereabouts as the afternoon wore on, but then she heard him talking to someone. At first she wasn't sure where he was, but she finally tracked him down to the garden, and as she approached, she was shocked to see him talking to a black snake which was coiled at his feet. Upon closer inspection she was even more startled to see that Martin had placed his cup of milk on the ground in front of the snake. Then, to her horror, Martin took his spoon and tapped the snake on the head, saying, "Don't drink all the milk. Eat some of the bread too."[2]

The story of Martin Houser and his snake is certainly a quaint piece of Americana, if it is true. However, similar stories have surfaced in New York state, and in other parts of Pennsylvania besides Greene, Fayette, and Centre Counties. This old legend about the child and a hungry snake has ancient roots indeed. The ideas behind the legend probably originated in Germany, most likely in the Middle Ages,

73

and were brought to this country by German immigrants in the early 1700's. The brothers Grimm, Jacob and Wilhelm, included the anecdote in their now-famous compilation of fairy tales, published in 1812, which they gathered in Germany's Black Forest. Their collection, which includes such popular tales as Hansel and Gretel, Little Red Riding Hood, and Rapunzel, are thought to date back to the dawn of story-telling in northern Europe.

In the Black Forest, during those times when enchanted maidens, powerful wizards, and magical beasts were believed to inhabit these impressive German mountains, there was, according to the Grimms' fairy tale, a mother who gave her little girl a bowl of milk and bread as an afternoon snack every day. The child would take her treat out to the yard and sit down there to eat. However, whenever she began to eat, a snake would slither out from a hole in the garden wall and crawl up to the bowl of milk. The snake then "dipped its little head in the dish, and ate with her".

The Grimms' fairy tale relates also that the child would sometimes call the snake if it didn't come forth right away. The snake was so grateful to the child for remembering to feed it that "it brought the child all kinds of pretty things from its hidden treasures - bright stones, pearls, and gold playthings." The snake would always drink the milk from the bowel, but never eat the bread. This didn't seem right to the child, and so "one day the child took its little spoon and struck the snake on the head with it, and said, 'Eat the bread-crumbs as well, little thing.'

The girl's mother overheard her daughter talking to someone, and walked out to see who it might be. When she saw the child tapping the snake with a spoon, she immediately picked up a piece of firewood and killed the reptile. After that, the little girl took ill and started to waste away. Then, according to the sad ending to the Grimms' tale, "the funeral bird began to cry in the night, and soon afterwards the child lay in her bier."[3]

These old ideas, that snakes will guard a treasure or can supernaturally cause a child to die, were once fully accepted as fact by people in different parts of Pennsylvania where the tale was known. Another version of this type of idea was once popular in Berks County where one old-timer there told me that "they say that about ginseng plants". "Snakes will guard the big ginseng plant. I go out hunting them and I always think of that, you know. When I find a big plant I loop around to see if there's a snake around. They claim they will protect them."[4]

Back in Centre County, in the Seven Mountains near Milroy, there was once a legend claiming that there is a treasure buried on top of a mountain along Route 322 known as Straley Knob. According to this story, the treasure at the top of this prominent peak is guarded by snakes, which become more numerous the closer the seeker gets to the fortune.

I've been to the top of Straley Knob and found no snakes or treasure. Even if riches are to be found in such places, it would certainly not be a very pleasurable experience to stumble into a writhing mass of snakes, especially in difficult terrain or in cramped quarters. However, such a thing can happen, as Sam Askey, the great pioneer panther hunter of Snow Shoe, Centre County, found out one day in the earlier part of the nineteenth century. On this particular occasion, Askey and Colonel John Holt, a fellow hunter, were returning from the "Big Moshannon licks" in the Allegheny Mountains. The men had killed some deer, and their horse was loaded with fresh venison. Just as they came to the top of a ridge on the north side of Black Moshannon

Creek near Snow Shoe, Askey's dog started barking excitedly. The little canine was somewhere off to the left and down at the bottom of a hill where it couldn't be seen, so Askey decided to investigate, probably thinking there might be an opportunity for a shot at more wild game.

Askey left Holt behind to watch the horse, and headed down the mountain. On the way to the dog, the intrepid hunter came upon a pile of large boulders. Rather than try to skirt around the extensive obstacle, he tried to make his way over it. He climbed up one particularly large rock, and then decided to jump down a distance of about five feet to the ground below. When he did so, he landed in the middle of a rattlesnake den. In recalling the incident, Askey claimed that there were so many snakes all around him "that every step I made I tramped upon them. It seemed to me like tramping over beef entrails on a butchering day."[5]

The great panther hunter didn't pause to see if the snakes were guarding a treasure, or protecting anything else for that manner. He did notice that they seemed to be moving towards an opening under the rock, but that's all he cared to see.

"You may be sure I handled myself lively," noted Askey . "I escaped from them without injury, excepting a brief sickness of stomach, occasioned by the stench which arose from the snakes. I did not stop to count nor to kill, and have no desire to come across another rattlesnake den. I soon found my dog, with a panther on a tree, which I shot, and returned with it to Holt, leaving the snake den off my route."[5]

Sam Askey's snakes didn't appear to be guarding any treasures, but the Grimm brothers' story about the child and the snake includes the ancient belief that snakes sometimes do just that. The snake in the Grimms' version of the tale had its own hidden valuables, from which it brought the child pearls and gold objects - an idea that appears to have come from ancient beliefs about dragons, which were usually imagined to be in the form of fire-breathing lizards or snakes, with scaly bodies, large bat-like wings, and barbed tails. Usually, however, the basic form of the dragon was snake-like, and its intentions portrayed as evil. Dragons, it was thought, sometimes guarded great wealth, including precious stones, items made of gold, etc. Beasts like this are common in Greek mythology, where it was believed one such animal guarded the golden apples in the mythical Garden of the Hesperides, and another, hundred-eyed monster, watched over the Golden Fleece sought by Jason and his Argonauts.

It also seems likely that the notion that killing the snake that was eating out of the child's bowl would lead to the death of the child probably arose from other old European tales about how dragons would carry off people and devour them. This may sound unlikely, but keep in mind that folk tales know no boundaries nor are they constrained by the passage of time. In fact, if the Grimms' story about the child and the snake could find a home here in Pennsylvania, who knows what other fairy tales did as well? Perhaps even Little Red Riding Hood could have been found here at one time too. I have yet to find a folk tale of a girl being chased by a wolf here in our mountains, but I've come close. The next story will be of interest to those who want to read more about just how "enchanted" Penn's Woods can be.

Jacob Houser's Old Millrace

Houserville, Centre County

LITTLE RED RIDING HOOD?

Stories of men being followed or actually attacked by wolves and panthers were once fairly common here in Pennsylvania, but similar tales about women seem to have been scarce indeed. One reason for this was, of course, that men spent more time out in the mountains, either hunting or working, than their women folk did during those days when mountain lions and wolves were not yet rare creatures here in the Keystone State. In other words, there were fewer opportunities for a woman to become the heroine of an episode like the popular German tale we know as Little Red Riding Hood.

On the other hand, there are a few folk tales that do preserve a memory of encounters women had with some fierce beasts of the forest - encounters that were probably as close as any of these heroines would have wanted to come to being a Pennsylvania version of the red-cloaked lass of Germany's Schwarzwald, or "Black Forest".

Without a doubt, there must have been at least one young lady here in Pennsylvania that was chased by a wolf or a pack of wolves during the last three-hundred years. Such a story would certainly make interesting reading today, but there don't seem to be any accounts like this that have survived - at least none that I've found. On the other hand, there are stories preserved of young ladies being chased by those big mountain cats that were known as panthers.

One such episode has been preserved in the folk tales of the northern Seven Mountains of Centre and Mifflin Counties. The event is said to have occurred in a remote valley formed by Kohler and First Mountains, Potter Township, Centre County. The heroine of the tale was Mary Auman Confer, wife of Benjamin Confer. She was born in 1854.

"They lived in Kohler Valley where the Mountain Acres camp is today," recalled Mary's granddaughter. "They ran a hotel there and had six children. She would walk out into the valley to work for someone and then would walk back at night. This one night she heard hollering up on the ridge. So she hollered back.

" Well, she thought it was kids hollering at her. Boys, some neighbor boys, that she thought were following her in the woods and just tormentin' her, you know. They were always playin' tricks on people. Yeah, that's what she thought, but it didn't happen to be. A panther followed her footsteps the wrong way, and when he did turn around and come back, why, she was at a farm house, and run in the gate and into the house just as he jumped over the fence.

" See, I was a kid when she told that, so I really don't know much more than I told you. I was too little to take this all in. It was just interesting to me that a panther followed my grandmother."[1]

Mary Confer never forgot that night when she was followed by the panther, and she also probably never forgot the lesson she learned the hard way, and which was common knowledge during Pennsylvania's panther days - a piece of wisdom that could still be heard in the Seven Mountains just ten years ago: "Well, they say if you make like them, they'll follow ya. I heard my dad sayin' still, if you hear them and make the same noise, why, they'd follow ya."[2]

There are very few authenticated accounts of panthers actually attacking humans here in Pennsylvania. In fact, Philip Tome, legendary wolf, panther, and elk hunter of northern Pennsylvania during the late 1700's and early 1800's, claimed that despite its reputation as a ferocious predator, the panther was "little feared by hunters".[3] Tome's book, entitled *Pioneer Life, or Thirty Years a Hunter*, is a volume that is still guaranteed to hold the interest of todays' devotees of the chase. Based on the knowledge he gained from his own thrilling experiences, Tome disavowed stories of panthers attacking men, noting that they "are undoubtedly without foundation".[3] The old hunter believed instead that panthers would go out of their way to avoid humans because, in his opinion, these fearsome animals had an "instinctive consciousness of man's superiority."[3]

Tome's observations would have provided little consolation to Mary Confer when she was being chased by the panther of Kohler Valley, nor would Tome's assessment have consoled Mariah Zettle one day when she became another Little Red Riding Hood of the Seven Mountains. Born in 1867, Mariah was a daughter of John Zettle of Decker Valley. The old Zettle homestead, traces of which are no longer visible today, is remembered as being "a house of square cut logs, with barn and out buildings".[4] Fortunately, Mariah's encounter with a panther has been preserved through oral history, and the tale has come down to us through her son, who wrote the story down for his children - an account which verifies that humans were not masters of, but merely intruders upon, the ridges that served as home to the beast once called "King of the Pennsylvania Forests".[5]

"She was the youngest in the family, which probably had something to do with the chores which befell her," began Mariah's adopted son. "I'd be very reluctant to assign such tasks to a young child, especially a girl, but she did have a wonderful and faithful dog, very aptly named "Watch", for a companion and helper.

"One of her weekly jobs was to walk the round trip of five or six miles to the store in Potters Mills and bring back a gallon of kerosene, or 'coal oil', as she called it. She remembered how tired her arms would get from lugging that oil and other items, and described some of the not-too-savory characters she met on these trips. But she never had any fear of them when her dog was with her.

"As the towns of New England had their 'commons', or public pastures, for their cattle, so, too, there was an area of natural semi-open fields a couple of miles from her house, where quite a few families pastured their stock. Much of the time her older brothers would drive the family cattle to this grazing area early in the morning, then go back in the evening and drive them home. But sometimes the job would be hers. Watch was the assistant they'd all take along, because he knew their cattle and would cut them out from the others and keep them bunched up and headed in the right direction, both to and from the pasture.

"In those days cattle were not de-horned the way they are today, and bulls were among the grazers too. But apparently no one really worried about sending a pre-teenage girl out on a job of this sort. And the way Mom told it - we'd describe it today as being 'a piece of cake'. All except one time, that is.

"One late autumn afternoon, she was heading homeward, daydreaming like young kids do. She was preceding the cattle by perhaps a hundred feet, which isn't a bad idea if you're barefooted, and Watch was last in the procession, keeping the herd moving and nipping at the heels of those that tended to stop to graze or stray off the path. As Mom's thoughts wandered from the shortening day, and how much earlier darkness was approaching, to the changing leaves, fading flowers, and so forth, her eyes caught a slight movement in the bush just a few feet from her. And there was this huge cat with frightening yellow eyes.

"Her instant reaction was a shrieking scream: 'Watch!'

And the response from the cat, which was probably as startled as she was, was a loud snarl and showing of his teeth. Time means nothing in such a happening, and Mom said the dog was there almost instantly, and immediately attacked the cat. She remembered how much larger the cat was than her dog, and he was a large mixed breed collie and shepherd.

"The fight must've really been terrible. She remembered the growls, screams, and thrashing around of both animals, but most of all, her running a short ways in terror. Then she realized she'd have to go back for the cattle or they'd scatter into the woods. So she forced herself to do this. She could hear the fading sounds of the fight still going on deeper off the path, but managed to get the frightened and excited cattle again started for home - but at a much slower pace without her dog.

"She said no one at home seemed worried about her after-dark arrival, as they knew her dog was with her. When she told them what had happened, her brothers took a lantern and gun and set out, but returned later without the dog.

"Days went by, and it's not hard to imagine the grief of the little girl. She was certain her dog had either been killed by the panther or had been found by her brothers so badly injured that they had shot him, though both had denied this. Offers from her dad to get her a new dog just seemed to make matters worse. And then one day, over a week later, Watch came dragging in. He was really ripped and chewed up, but the care and doctoring of the whole family eventually brought him around again. And both he and his owner were able to resume the obligations expected of them.

"One of the highlights of the social life of the young people of that era was to attend evangelistic services, or camp meetings, in groups. The walk to the meetings at twilight was probably a lark, but the trip back in the darkness was sort of scary, even considering the safety-in-numbers idea. And I remember her saying that they would walk to some of these over near what I think she called Georges Valley.

"One bright moonlight night, they observed a set of eyes in the woods near the road. Usually a couple of rocks thrown by the boys would put the flight in the animal they discovered, but on this occasion the rocks just elicited growls and snarls from the large, dimly-visible, beast. So they got out of there quick. One of the boys told his father about the incident, and the next day they found a mangled carcass of a deer at the spot.

"A few days later another resident shot a panther very close by, and the old-timers allowed that it was the biggest they'd ever seen in those parts. Mom saw the remains of that panther, and she always said it wasn't nearly as big as the one attacked by her dog."[4]

Although the preceding tales may have been a disappointment to those readers who thought they were going to read an honest-to-goodness Pennsylvania version of the Grimm's fairy tale called Little Red Riding Hood, I hope that they won't feel too slighted. However, if the tales themselves don't provide enough of a thrill or fail to lift the reader to the level of satisfaction that he or she had hoped, then there is one thing guaranteed to do so. Merely take a ride, or, better yet, a walk, through these same valleys where Mary Confer and Mariah Zettle were stalked by beasts that were as intimidating to them as the "big bad wolf" was to Little Red Riding Hood. These places haven't changed too much since those early times. In fact, since coyotes can be found in these same valleys today, there may just be a panther or two lingering in the brush alongside the roads that wind back into the mountains - mountains whose stories are almost as enchanting as those fairy tales once told in Germany's Black Forest.

} BURNED AT THE STAKE {

In the summer of 1779, General John Sullivan was instructed to take 5,000 Colonial troops from Easton, Pennsylvania, and follow the Susquehanna River straight into the heart of the Six Nations' territory. Tired of numerous Indian raids upon the frontier, General George Washington ordered Sullivan to burn the Indians' houses, destroy their crops and their cattle, and to lay to waste anything else that the Indians might need to survive through the next winter. Prior to this time the typical style of warfare between whites and Indians had been mostly guerilla tactics and hand-to-hand struggles on a small scale. But now the level of combat was raised to a new dimension.

Indians of the Six Nations had never contended with a force like this, nor had such an army ever been seen along the banks of the Susquehanna before. Although strong enough to contend with almost any Indians they were likely to encounter, this impressive legion could not have been successful at keeping its whereabouts a secret. People for miles up river must have known they were coming, with five thousand voices alternately interrupting the stillness of the vast virgin forests and the sound of ten thousand marching feet reverberating down the wilderness trails. Intimidating as the army was, every individual soldier had to be constantly alert for signs of the enemy.

Although a deadly Indian ambush could always be waiting around the next bend in the trail, flashes of light from the polished steel of bayonets catching the suns rays, and strains of martial music rising from numerous fifes and drums must have made the cheerless forests seem less somber. In the river alongside the trail, one hundred and fifty supply boats carried the cannons and materials that were essential to the success of the mission. At sundown the leaders of this human juggernaut would pick a spot on the river bank to camp for the night. Here the soldiers would build their many cooking fires and watch fires, creating a brilliant spectacle "stretching for miles along the river".[1]

Fortunately for the American cause, but not so fortunate for the Indians of the Six Nations, Sullivan's huge army accomplished the task it had set out to do. The Indian towns of Tioga, Chemung, Catherine's Town, Kendaia, Canandaigua, and other villages, fell before Sullivan's unrelenting and terrible sword. Abundant fields of squash, peas, pumpkins, beans, peppers, and maize were all destroyed as well. At Newtown, near present-day Elmira, New York, the Indians and their Tory and British allies were handed an especially devastating defeat - one which was described as the worst the Indians had ever received in the east.

The Indians had always wished for another stupendous victory like their defeat of British General Braddock, which occurred near Fort Duquesne in July of 1755 during the French and Indian War, but these dreams were not to be realized at Newtown when the Indians' attempted ambush was turned against them. It was also a particularly bad loss for the British because their Indian allies had been raising horses for the British army here. It was as true then as it was later, during the first World War, that " you can replace a man, but you can't replace a horse".[2] Sullivan, accordingly, killed every Indian horse he could find. Today the memory of this terrible slaughter is perpetuated in the name of the town that grew up here: Horseheads, New York.

For years after Sullivan's victory, the Indians harbored the sting of defeat in their hearts. The Senecas held George Washington particularly responsible for their losses since he was, after all, "The Father of His Country". To the Senecas he was known by another name, that of "Town Destroyer". Even ten years after the destruction of their villages, the Senecas would say that whenever that name was heard "our women look behind them and turn pale, and our children cling close to their mothers."[3]

It was victories like Sullivan's at Newtown that added to the British conviction that Americans were among the best marksmen in the world - a statement that was not without some foundation. "Kentucky" rifles, which were actually invented and made in Pennsylvania, were more reliable and more accurate than firearms made in Europe, largely due to the rifling that Pennsylvania gunsmiths added to the inside of rifle barrels. These innovative rifle makers were rewarded with a steady stream of customers. Every man was a hunter in those days, and young boys were taught how to shoot and hunt from the time they could hold a musket.

Hunters had their own favorite guns, oftentimes one for deer and one for turkeys, and the abundance of game gave everyone plenty of opportunity to sharpen their marksmanship. They became so good, in fact, that one Englishman, in a report sent back to the British government, reckoned that Americans were "the best marksmen in the world".[4] This same gentleman expanded upon his assessment, noting that "in marching through the woods, one thousand of these riflemen would cut to pieces ten thousand of your best troops."[4] This statement was, of course, unintentionally prophetic and, as British troops were later to learn, not exaggerated in the least. It didn't take King George's red-coated battalions long to develop a healthy fear of the Pennsylvania "shirt tail men", and "their cursed twisted barrel guns, the most fatal widow and orphan makers in the world."[4]

General Sullivan had some of the best of these "widow and orphan maker" riflemen with him on his expedition. Included in this select group was Tim Murphy, one of Captain John Lowden's elite riflemen from Northumberland County. Murphy was credited as being the sharpshooter who killed General Frazer at the battle of Saratoga in 1777, thus greatly influencing the outcome of that battle. The skills of the other riflemen from Pennsylvania were just as impressive. One witness to their uncanny accuracy said they could consistently hit a mark "with great certainty at 200 yards distance", killing British soldiers and officers "even at more than double the distance of a common musket shot."[4]

Other Pennsylvania riflemen may have been able to match Tim Murphy's marksmanship, but it was Murphy's luck that surpassed that of most of his compatriots. Several incidents in Murphy's life indicate that he must have had "the luck of the Irish" with him at times, but there was one outstanding tale that would seem to prove it. In this particular instance some Indians were pursuing Murphy, who was carrying a very unusual gun for that day, a double-barreled musket. The fleet-footed Indians were gaining on him at every step, and so Murphy finally turned and shot one. This gave him some time to duck behind a tree and reload the barrel he had just fired. After that, he raced off once again, but the Indians were soon on his heels. Murphy stopped short once more, then turned and fired, killing another Indian. This action delayed his pursuers a second time, but they soon resumed the chase, and were almost upon him again when he shot a third warrior. After this shot the remaining Indians ran off as if frightened away. Years later Murphy found out that the braves that were chasing him thought that he had "a great medicine of a gun that would shoot forever," because he fired three times and they had not seen him reload even once.[5]

Murphy survived several close calls like this, but many of his contemporaries did not. Among his less fortunate compatriots were

Jacob Shedacre and Thomas Van Doran, both of whom had been with him at Saratoga. These two men had, just the year before Sullivan's campaign, been attacked and killed by five Indians in Penns Valley, Centre County. Today, along the township road known as "Indian Lane", there is a monument placed at the spot where these two brave soldiers fought their last fight.

There were also two other Murphy comrades whose luck was not much better than that of Shedacre and Van Doran of Indian Lane. These two other men were brothers John and Thomas Boyd from Northumberland, Pennsylvania. Both were personal friends of Murphy's, but only Thomas joined him when he went off with Sullivan's army.

An expedition as large as Sullivan's required huge quantities of supplies, and at least some of these may have been stored at Sunbury and then moved up the West Branch on flatboats. According to Northumberland County legend, it was at Sunbury that Thomas Boyd joined Sullivan's army, and he was followed here, so says the same legend, by a pregnant young girl who claimed that he was the child's father. Thomas refused to acknowledge the child as his own, and so wouldn't marry the distraught young lady, despite her frantic pleas. Finally she cursed him. "I hope the Indians burn you", were her parting words to the faithless father.[2] Later, in a moment of compassion, she might have asked herself why she hadn't wished for a lesser punishment.

After Boyd and his fellow soldiers reached the Genessee Valley, he was ordered to take out a scouting party and search for signs of the enemy. Boyd's contingent of twenty-four men soon discovered the Indian village of Little Castle nestled along the river, and here they killed and scalped two Indians. Having temporarily satisfied their thirst for scalps, the Boyd party started back to the main body of troops. The tension must have been unbearable for the men. They were in hostile territory, and they didn't know if the enemy was near or not. At any moment a screaming band of warriors, intent upon revenge, could descend upon them with deadly fury. When it came, the attack was swift and devastating, perhaps sounding as though the furies of hell itself had been unleashed upon the earth.

Fourteen of Boyd's twenty-four men were killed in the first moments of the attack. These were lucky men compared to sergeant Michael Parker and Lt. Boyd, who were captured and unmercifully tortured. The remaining eight soldiers, including Tim Murphy, were lucky enough to escape somehow. Murphy and the others made it back to the main force, where they reported on the fate of their friends. An accelerated march was ordered in hopes that the two captives could be rescued, but when the troops reached the spot where Boyd and Parker had been captured, they found the mens' mangled remains lying beside flaming torture fires.

Today in New York's Genessee Valley there is a state historical marker commemorating the "Torture Tree". The marker's inscription reads: "This wayside shrine marks the place where, on Sept. 14, 1779, two young soldiers of the Revolution, Lt. Thomas Boyd and Sgt Michael Parker met death undaunted in the line of duty after lingering torture. They marked with their blood the western limits of the state of New York in the great struggle for American freedom."

So it would seem that during that balmy September day in 1779, Tim Murphy's luck had been with him once again and Thomas Boyd's pregnant young lady got her wishes. But there is a sequel to this story, one that involves Thomas Boyd's brother John. As happened so often in those days, Captain John Boyd and his company of about forty rangers were ambushed in Blair County near the headwaters of the Juniata River's Raystown Branch, about two years after Thomas' death. Captain Boyd was wounded and captured, despite a powerful struggle.

The young captain did manage to escape momentarily, but he was recaptured and struck on the head three times with a tomahawk, each blow causing a terrible gash in his skull. Despite his ghastly wounds, Boyd and other prisoners were carried off into the wilderness. When they got to the mouth of the Sinnemahoning Creek in Cameron County, the Indians decided to kill a man named Ross, who could travel no further. Boyd was forced to watch the man's torture, and after it was over the Indians prepared to do the same with Boyd. Resigning himself to his fate, Boyd began singing a plaintive Masonic song he knew. The Indians were surprised by this action, and actually stopped their fiendish work until Boyd was done singing. When he stopped, an Oneida squaw came forward and claimed him as her son. It was customary for Indian braves to accept such adoptions as prerogatives of Indian women who had lost their own sons in battle, and so not a single man interfered in this case.

The Oneida squaw nursed Boyd back to health and watched over him the remainder of the journey, which ended in Quebec. About a year later, Boyd and several other fellow prisoners were released and sent to Philadelphia. Boyd never forgot the Oneida squaw whose actions spared him the agonies of a horrible death. He often sent her gifts and even visited her one time, "personally thanking her for saving his life".[6]

When comparing the story of John Boyd with that of his brother it would almost appear, if the legend about Thomas has any factual basis, that fate, through one of its ironic twists, was somehow trying to restore some balance of order to the universe. If this conclusion were true it would then seem that the method by which fate was trying to accomplish its means was through a woman. For it was a woman, so says the legend, that was Thomas's nemesis, while it was another woman, according to history, who was his brother's savior. But just how true is the legend? The story about Thomas and the pregnant girl appears to have migrated to Sunbury from New York State. In the Schoharie Valley of that state, the tale was widely accepted as historical fact and preserved in its historical chronicles.

These records state that during the summer of 1778 Thomas Boyd was encamped in the Schoharie Valley with other American troops. Here he supposedly met and courted Cornelia, "the beautiful daughter of Bartholomew Becker."[7] Cornelia became pregnant during the courtship, and she entered the soldiers' camp in an hysterical state the day the troops were preparing to leave to join Sullivan's army. She found Boyd in the middle of all the confusion, and angrily demanded that he marry her before he left. His glib words and false promises were not enough anymore, and in a fit of desperate anger Cornelia cursed him, saying "if he went off without marrying her, she hoped he would be cut in pieces by the Indians."[7] Just then Boyd's commanding officer rode up and ordered him to delay no more, the time to march had come. Embarrassed by being reprimanded by a girl, and in front of his own commander, Boyd pulled out his sword and pointed it at Cornelia, saying he would run her through if she didn't leave right away.

If these were the actions of Thomas Boyd, then perhaps he's not as deserving of a monument as other brave soldiers who died just as nobly. Apparently local records show that the unwed Cornelia Becker did give birth to a baby girl. Other accounts note that local gossips whispered amongst themselves about the baby's father. Several opinions must have surfaced, but popular belief was that the father was

Thomas Boyd, the soldier Cornelia had confronted in the army camp. It can only be hoped that the false-hearted lover of the legend was not Thomas Boyd, but instead was some other soldier who never again gave a young girl reason to wish that anyone would be burned at the stake.

RIDDEN

Pennsylvania's folk beliefs once included the idea that witches would break into a farmer's barn at night and ride one of his horses just to torment the defenseless beast. The next morning the farmer would come to the barn and find his horse all lathered up and tired, as though it had been ridden for hours. Further "proof" of the witch's nocturnal antics would be masses of tiny hair knots in the horses' mane and tail. These numerous tangles were almost always impossible to separate, and they were so annoying and so baffling that many people once believed they could only have been put there by a witch as she took the animal on wild rides through dark hollows and mist-shrouded forests bathed in the unearthly light of a full moon. At least that was the theory often proposed to explain where the knots came from. After all, they hadn't been there when the horse was bedded down for the night, and so a witch must have put them there.

Of course there is a logical explanation that accounts for the tangles that appear in horses' manes and tails overnight, but even less than a hundred years ago many people still attributed the knots to witch riding. As a result, there were steps that people took to insure that witches could not even enter their barns at all. One popular way to do this was to place a "witch paper" behind the horseshoe that was a common good luck ornament nailed above the barn door. Another method used to repel witches from barns was to carve magical symbols in the beams and rafters of the barn itself. Of the two methods, the witch paper was probably the quickest and easiest. Those who elected to use such papers would get them from the local powwower, or *braucher*, who would perform the necessary magical steps needed to prepare these protective scripts.

More often than not, the *braucher* would write special symbols or occult sentences on an ordinary piece of paper and then probably recite some equally obscure incantations over it before pronouncing it ready to use. Each *braucher* had his own favorite inscriptions to put on a witch paper, but many of them relied on passages from John George Hohman's book of "mysterious arts and remedies" entitled *Pow-wows, or The Long-Lost Friend.* This little handbook was touted as a collection of cures for numerous ailments and problems, with the "cures" being supernatural symbols and sentences that could be used to ward off evil.

Published sometime in the early 1800's, this popular reference was, said the author, "collected with much pain and trouble from all parts of the world", and was based upon "a work published by a Gypsy" and on "secret writings", including that of early "authority" Albertus Magnus.[1] Typical of the recommendations in the book is a charm that was to be written on a piece of paper and fed to a farmer's cattle by mixing it in with their feed. The charm was to be written in this way:[2]

```
S A T O R
A R E P O
T E N E T
O P E R A
R O T A S
```

Another charm, guaranteed to "protect and free all persons and animals from witchcraft", was to be placed upon a piece of paper and kept in the barn or house. The inscription was to read as follows:

Trotterhead, I forbid thee my house and premises; I forbid thee my horse and cow stable; I forbid thee my bedstead, that thou mayest not breathe upon me; breathe into some other house, until thou hast ascended every hill, until thou hast counted every fence-post, and until thou hast crossed every water. And thus dear day may come again into my house, in the name of God the Father, the Son, and the Holy Ghost. Amen. "[3]

A witch paper with these very lines penciled upon it was once owned by antique dealer Lester Zettle of Georges Valley, Gregg Township, Centre County. The antiquary was always willing to show the paper to interested parties, and he would explain how he had found it, and many others quite like it, hidden in secret spots of older houses where he was invited to appraise antiques. According to Zettle, families would place the papers behind the horseshoes hanging over their barn doors and over the doors leading into their homes. The idea was that people needed to be protected from witches' spells just as much as their cattle and their horses in the barn. For there were witches, so it was believed, who not only enjoyed tormenting horses by riding them until they were almost dead, but who also liked doing the same thing to humans.

Years ago, tales of witches riding people could probably have been found in many remote mountainous sections of the state, but these types of tales seemed to linger longest in certain places, including the Tuscarora Mountains of Juniata, Perry and Mifflin Counties. Anyone who has ever traveled over, or done any hunting in, the Tuscarora State Forest knows how rugged and challenging these towering peaks can be. Even from a distance, the bold outline of Tuscarora Mountain seems to rise to an incredible height into the heavens. Sunny days bring the stately hill into sharper focus, but despite the best weather there always appears to be a mist which lends a blue cast to the mountain. Then on rainy days the summit is often obscured by clouds, and white pockets of fog can be seen rising from or hanging on to the sides of the majestic peak. Perhaps it was this mist that helped make the region a storehouse of legend and romance, by reminding people of tales from other mountain ranges - the Blue Mountains of Schuylkill County or the Hartz Mountains of Germany.

The romantic stories and legends that were once told in Germany's Black Forest, and in other mountainous parts of that country, are among the most treasured fairy tales in the world. However, there was also a dark side to the accounts that were brought here from Germany, and included among this set of yarns are many tales of the supernatural and of witchcraft. For example, on particularly damp days, when dense clouds of white vapor would rise from the top of the Blue Mountain, Pennsylvania Dutch settlers of Schuylkill County once believed that the mists came from cauldrons of metzel soup being brewed by "demon wolves".[4] No doubt these same German settlers had their witch stories that they would tell, and perhaps it was one of these same tales that found its way to Tuscarora Mountain.

The Tuscarora Indians had many legends of their own about these forests and mountains that eventually were named after them, but the white men who settled here brought their own tales along, and one of these was a story about how witches would ride people.

"I never heard anybody say that they changed them into horses," recalled one man who had been told the witch tales of the area, "although I wouldn't have been surprised to hear that. What they did was to saddle them, bridle them, and ride 'em, and spur them, and whip them, and tie them up, and slap them, and make them stand over, just as though they were horses. They'd ride them over hill and dale, and hitch them up in front of some big house, with a blaze of lights in the window, where some witches' frolic was going on.

"These witches, or this witch, would go in there and spend all night reveling around, come out, and ride him back home again. And in the morning they'd be found exhausted and half dead, with the marks of the rowels and the spurs in their sides, and the whip marks.

"So they knew they'd been ridden by witches. Now I never heard anybody tell me how that spell was broken or how they could avoid that, but there were several people that mentioned this to me, and I gathered it was a rather common idea that it could be done. It's funny about this. You don't often find that somebody, himself, has had the experience. It's always somebody else that he knew."[5]

Anecdotes like this had their origins in Europe, where they were not only popular in Germany, but also in England, Denmark, and Iceland. In England, for example, a story was told that a man was once lying on his bed and a witch entered the room. She threw a "magic halter" over his head, and he immediately turned into a horse. The witch then mounted him and rode off to a witches' revel. Here he had to wait, unless he could find a way to slip the halter over the witch's head. If he could not accomplish this, the witch would then remount him when she was leaving the frolic and gallop him unmercifully back to his home. If he did manage to slip the halter over her head, she would change into a horse, and he could then ride her "almost to death".[6]

So fantastic were some of these tales that it's a wonder that anyone could believe them, but the stories probably were lavishly embellished as they were told and retold. Another English tale which falls in this category was that of the man who bought a horse, not knowing it was a "witch-mare". The horse was shod like any other horse, but when the man removed its bridle, the horse turned back into his wife, "with a horseshoe nailed to each hand and foot"![6]

No fantastic stories like this can be found in Pennsylvania anymore, or maybe they never were told here, but sixty years ago Pennsylvania Dutchmen of Berks, Lancaster, and Lehigh Counties would point out circular spots in fields where nothing would grow and call them "witch rings", defining them as the spots where witches "held their revels".[7] However, even that belief has gone the way of other old superstitions, just as witches seem to have ridden off into the sunset, either on horses or on humans turned into horses. Nonetheless, modern day science may now be able to explain where those "witch-mares" came from in the first place.

Historians have noted that at the Salem witch trials, held in Salem Massachusetts in 1692, some of the "witnesses" against accused witches claimed they were turned into horses and ridden by the witch. Jurors, and most everyone else, apparently believed such testimonies were true, probably due in part to the emotionally charged atmosphere and, maybe in some cases, a willingness to settle old grudges. However there was also a deep-seated belief that witchcraft was real, and that witches could turn men into horses whenever they pleased. There must've been some very strong reasons why such beliefs and such fantastic stories could last so long and influence people so greatly. In fact, modern studies suggest there may be a basis for the ideas after all.

Among the most unusual folk tales ever studied by scholars of folklore would have to be the episodes that one folklorist has called "The terror that comes in the night".[8] Stories of awful nightmares involving an imp-like creature that sits on a sleeper's chest and renders him immobile, and then tries to draw the unconscious person's soul from his body, have been documented for centuries. The dreamers' descriptions of their nightmares are always strikingly similar in their details. Basically, however, the main elements of the experience seem to be an unfathomably black imp that sits upon the dreamer's chest, complete paralysis over the entire body, and a horrible feeling that the imp is trying to draw the dreamer's soul right out of his body, or her body, for the experience has been reported by both sexes.

This nightmarish experience has been around for hundreds of years, which is proven by Henry Fuseli's famous work of art entitled "The Nightmare". Created in 1781, the painting depicts a sleeping woman sprawled across her bed. Sitting on her chest is an evil-looking imp, and peering into the bedroom through a partially-opened door is the head of a horse. The elements portrayed in Fuseli's painting correspond closely to the images, sensations, and emotions felt by those who have experienced "the terror that comes in the night", and, it may also be said, quite closely to the predicaments talked about in the tales of witch riding.

Scary as this all my sound, science has come up with some logical theories that can explain several elements of the night terror experience. Psychiatrists, for example, have identified some people who occasionally have bouts of what is called sleep paralysis. In these brief episodes the sleeper becomes paralyzed, due to an unusual bodily process, just as they are falling asleep or just as they are waking up. Typical of this abnormal sleep behavior are the "vivid and terrifying hallucinations"[9] that are seen by the sleepers. Similarly, it has been established that people with narcolepsy, the inability to remain awake, have experiences that lead to hallucinations, which are also "usually unpleasant".[10]

Although it's nice to know that science may have finally discovered the basis for another old witch tale, it's also sad in a way. It's too bad that such explanations weren't available during the Salem witch trials. If this knowledge had been around at that time, then maybe people wouldn't have been as likely to condone the executions of innocent victims who were convicted on the belief that they could change someone else into a horse and ride them until they dropped.

DEAD FOR THREE DAYS

When Confederate forces, under General Robert E. Lee, began their second invasion of the Keystone State in June of 1863, residents of the Cumberland Valley soon realized that the winds of war had blown their way once again. Rebel forces had not ventured into Pennsylvania since J.E.B. Stuart's invasion in October of 1862. But now the green valleys and dusty brown roads of York, Franklin and Adams Counties were streaked with lines of butternut and grey - the colors of Confederate soldiers' uniforms. The columns of marching troops stirred up clouds of dust that signaled their approach, but it was not the dust that often alerted residents that the Rebels were coming.

According to Eighty-nine year old Adams countian Paul Boring, who heard the story from his father and grandmother, "In the days of the Civil War the Rebels come down over [present-day] Route 30, and they took over the city of York. They had sentinels that they'd send out to pick up supplies, and they went north into the village of Rossville [York County]. Along the northwest side of the Conewago Creek was most of the farms. The other side was hills and what have you. So they went down through there to pick up their horses and raid the smoke houses. There's where they'd get their hams, but they wanted flour too. In those days their flour was in bags, twenty-five pound bags. My great grandfather was down Conewago Creek - from Route 74 it would'a been three miles. He said you could hear the Rebels' horses going on the road, you know, and they knew they were coming. So they'd get their horses out of their barnyards and stables, and swim them across the Conewago Creek, to the hilly country and the pine trees, and hide them."

"And some of the Rebels give 'em a hard time. They said, 'Hey, you don't make all that manure with the small amount of horses you got in that stable.' See, they were pretty cagy too. My dad said that his father told him that the Rebels wanted to take a mare from my great grandfather. I believe it was probably heavy in foal. But the Rebel was gonna take his horses, and he walked on with this Rebel tryin' to lead his horse. And he grabbed him by the leg, and they had differences of opinion. So my dad said his grandpa grabbed a stone and said, 'You take that mare back or I'll knock the brains out of you."[1]

Robert E. Lee's troops didn't have much time to plunder the locals of Adams County. In a matter of days, in that same county, the Rebel forces found themselves face-to-face with Federal troops at a little country town named Gettysburg. Volumes have been written on the events that occurred during the three days' battle that occurred at Gettysburg on July first, second, and third, 1863, and it would seem that there's not much else that can be told about that great engagement. However, descendants of soldiers who fought at Gettysburg remember stories that have been passed down from generation to generation over the last one-hundred and thirty years - stories which have never been preserved on the printed page.

Oral history like this, although interesting, loses its freshness and first-hand color when it is passed down from person to person over the decades. In other words, the closer the teller of such stories is to the man who lived them, the more thrilling the tales are likely to sound to the listener. If this theory is true, then Alverta March's anecdotes should prove highly entertaining to the reader. Mrs. March, a native of Franklintown, Adams County, was born in 1903. A daughter of Michael Sloan, who fought at the battle of Gettysburg, the ninety-one year old lady was, in 1994, the only surviving child of a Civil War veteran in the state of Pennsylvania.

According to Mrs. March, her father was born in Dublin, Ireland, in 1841, and was 62 years old when she was born. The wide age difference between veterans and their children was not that unusual for many Civil war vets, who often married women much younger than themselves. Michael Sloan enlisted in the Fifth Maryland Infantry, U. S. Regulars, during the Civil War, and saw no action until July, 1863, when his unit became involved in the big skirmish at Gettysburg. On the evening of the battle's first day, the young twenty-two year old was assigned lookout duty near the pile of huge boulders called Devil's Den. It was here, at this key battlefield landmark, that Michael Sloan had an experience that he would often recall in his later years.

Mrs. March tells the story in both her words and her father's:

"He said, 'One morning it was breakin' daylight, and I saw a fella across on the other side of this wagon road through Devil's Den, and we were both aimin' at one another.'

"And so, you know, the Irish were Catholic. So he said, 'I formed a cross over me, and he done the same.'

"And the enemy put his gun down, and pop put his gun down. And the enemy said he hoped he lives to get home and see his wife and two children. Pop says, 'I hope you do too.' They shook hands and parted. It always touches me when I think of it. Pop said they would'a both been court-martialed if they'd been seen."

Twenty four hours later, the young Irishman from Dublin had reason to wish that he had been court-martialed the day before. On the second day of the battle, Michael Sloan was shot through the head with a minnie ball that entered his forehead at the hairline and came out behind his ear.

"I often think of him layin' there in the hot sun, on the second, and third of July," Mrs. March continued. "He laid there on the battlefield. It was war goin' on, and nobody had time to pick 'em all up. Pop said they picked up the best ones that they thought would live, and the ones they thought would die, they left lay. He must've had a strong constitution. He had Irish blood in him!"[2]

Mike Sloan bore the scars of his gunshot wound the rest of his life, a reminder of the battle of Gettysburg. However, there were other souvenirs as well, such as the wrist bone that stuck out at an odd angle, the missing jar containing three-hundred dollars, and the bad dreams. Had the young Irishman known all the ordeals his military service would lead him through he might not have enlisted in the first place. However, Sloan's reasons for signing up were not entirely based on patriotism or a yearning for adventure.

Mike was a hired boy on a farm when the war broke out, and the farmer's son got drafted. The farmer didn't want his son to go off to war, and so he offered his hired man a fee to go instead. Hiring someone to take your place in the draft was legal during the Civil War, "so pop volunteered", explained Mrs. March. "They gave pop three hundred dollars to go, and he buried it in a glass jar at a tree. And when he come home from the army the tree was cut down, and he never got his three hundred. That story he used to talk about all the time".

Private Sloan somehow managed to survive the Civil War, and he did eventually get some monetary rewards for his services. His veteran's pension from the Federal Government rose to thirty dollars a month in his later years, and the extra income was a source of amusement to the old vet, who used to say, "A dollar a day, work or play."

Although MIke Sloan's pension dollars increased over the years, the number of Civil War veterans steadily decreased until only a handful remained. However, Sloan managed to stay close to the scenes of his war days, eventually buying a farm near Biglerville, Adams County. The farm was within ten miles of the famous battlefield. But after a time there were no fellow soldiers to share memories with anymore, and perhaps it was for this reason that Mike Sloan seemed to enjoy more frequent trips to the battlefield as he grew older. He and his daughters became regular visitors on Sunday afternoons, riding over the former war zone in their horse and buggy. Michael felt a very strong attachment to the place where he had almost died, and no one could keep him away from there, although some men once tried.

Mrs. March was riding along in the horse and buggy that particular Sunday afternoon in 1910, and when they got to the battlefield they encountered a group of ten or twelve officials who were in the midst of a discussion, apparently planning some ceremonial maneuvers. "And they ordered us off the battlefield," said Mrs. March, recalling the incident as though it were only yesterday. "Pop stopped the buggy and jumped out, and he said, 'You S- B- you,' he said, 'don't you order me off of this ground. I laid here for three days and two nights among the dead and dyin'. They shook hands, and they talked. I was lookin' for pop to hit him."

Maybe the daytime trips to the Gettysburg Battlefield were a source of comfort to the old soldier. He perhaps merely wanted to reassure himself that the soldiers that died here were properly buried and at peace; when night fell Mike Sloan was sometimes not so sure if they were or not. "He used to get dreams at night," his daughter continued, "and I'd hear him carryin' on. And he used to always say the next morning, when I asked him what was wrong, 'The dead men were layin' around my bed like black birds.' I guess they'd dream of that stuff if you were in them battles."

Bad dreams didn't prevent Mike Sloan from keeping a few souvenirs of his Civil War days. In an old trunk he preserved a few pieces of 'hardtack', the hard biscuits that were a common staple of a soldier's diet, a canteen, and other relics. He also had his Civil War musket. The old war-time keepsakes are now gone, dispersed to persons unknown, and Mrs. March bemoaned the fact that they were no longer a part of the family. "But I didn't think about it as a kid," she noted. "I didn't think about keepin' those things. Pop ought'a thought of it. I often think now, Pop should'a thought of that stuff." We can all probably sympathize with Mrs. March's feelings of loss, but at least Mike Sloan left us with his stories - memories which preserve details of the kinds of people who fought to make this country the democratic bastion it is today.

Footnote: Mrs. Alverta March died in October, 1994.

Devil's Den (1863)

This view of Devil's Den, with Little Round Top in the background,
was taken by the Weavers of Hanover, Pennsylvania. Obviously a staged sh
the 'dead' soldiers were most likely Gettysburg veterans who were asked to
pose for the photo when they returned here in November of 1863 for the
dedication of the Soldiers' National Cemetery. The Weavers took many
pictures of the battlefield and sold them as stereographic views.
Courtesy Pennsylvania Historical and Museum Commission ,
Archives and Manuscripts (MG 218 Photo Collection)

Devil's Den (1996)

& Michael Sloan (1841 - 1926)

This modern day view of Devil's Den was taken from the same angle as the

photo on the previous page. The 'soldiers' here are Boy Scouts , who

added a livelier atmosphere to the rocks compared to the soldiers of 1863.

MOLLIE MAGUIRE MEMORIES

Oil, natural gas, and coal were once referred to as the "Pennsylvania triplets", due to the prevalence of these natural resources in the Keystone State.[1] Each of these energy sources spawned an industry dedicated to removing them from the ground, and as these industries grew so did the legends, folk tales, and interesting anecdotes about the people and places associated with them. However, it seems that coal mining has generated more such stories than either of the other two industries combined. Maybe it is the dangerous working conditions associated with coal mining, or perhaps just the type of people who do the work, but from the stories of Philip Ginder, said to be the discoverer of anthracite in Northampton County, to the tales of ghosts in the mines, there are enough stories and story types to entertain almost anyone.

Many of the narratives of the coal mining industry are not the most pleasant to hear. This is especially true of the accounts about the disasters that occurred when mines caved in, killing all the miners below. Poor working conditions and absence of safe mining practices led to many deaths, and it was the mine owners who often sacrificed miners' lives rather than spend money to fix unsafe conditions. It was just such disasters and conditions that gave birth to an organization of men who have been described as victims by some, and criminals by others. Known as Mollie Maguires, these men introduced what can only be described as a reign of terror into the coal mining regions of northeastern Pennsylvania in the last half of the 1860's and most of the 1870's. So sensationalistic were some of the Mollies' actions that the people of the northeastern Pennsylvania coal regions can still remember

110

tales of the Mollie Maguires. Although the Mollies' main headquarters was in Shenandoah, Schuylkill County, they managed to commit murders, sabotage trains, burn collieries and wreck bridges throughout neighboring anthracite coal counties, including Carbon, Columbia, and Northumberland. Many mine bosses and superintendents lived in terror, hoping they never received one of the Mollies' "Coffin Notices", a piece of paper decorated with a picture of a coffin or with a skull and cross-bones and an order to leave the area or die. The objective of the Mollies was to intimidate the mine owners to such an extent that they would improve the working conditions of the miners and pay them more as well. In that sense the Mollies were forerunners of the UMW (United Mine Workers') Union, which would not be fully organized for another twenty years in 1890.

It could be argued that the UMW might have taken longer to be founded if it weren't for desperate actions by men like the Mollie Maguires in Pennsylvania. On the other hand, it might be said that the Mollies did more harm to the miners' labor movement than it did good. This latter contention could be easily supported given the fact that the Mollies did not confine their attacks to just mining officials. Oral history and folk stories of the anthracite regions of Pennsylvania contain tales of attacks on innocent people by Mollie Maguires whose only purpose seemed to be to terrorize whole counties in order to get their message across. Not all Mollies engaged in this kind of vendetta, but it cannot be denied that a criminal element did exist in the organization. However, the sad fact is that the mine owners, themselves, were not "choir boys" either. The difference between the owners and the miners was that the owners had power and wealth, while the miners, in those days of no labor laws and no unions, could only resort to violence.

This type of violence is, of course, familiar to us today when we read of the terroristic attacks that occur in Northern Ireland, Israel, and other such places. Somewhat like the Mollies, today's terrorists don't care whose life they may take just to publicize their grievances. In all fairness to the Mollies, however, the mine owners were not much better. The murders the Mollies committed were rightly condemned, and the perpetrators were relentlessly hunted down. However, when miners died in cave-ins that were caused by the refusal of mine owners to spend money to insure that men would not have to work in such unsafe conditions, there did not seem to be any retribution that the mine owners had to worry about, at least in this world. Moreover, at least one coal company had its own police force that was charged with keeping the company's employees in line. As it turned out, however, the Coal and Iron Police of the Philadelphia and Reading Coal Company were nothing more than a bunch of bullies with their own terrorist tactics, and, consequently, were universally despised by the miners.

Frustration and desperation were constant companions of the average miner. He worked for paltry wages in absolutely miserable conditions under constant fear of death. When he came home, he saw his family living in deplorable hovels with barely enough to eat at times. Food was available at the company store, but the more a miner bought there the deeper in debt to the company he got; his wages were not even enough to cover his day-to-day living expenses. Desperate men eventually do desperate things and some Mollies finally decided to take some drastic actions to improve their lot.

There were probably both exaggerated and fictitious stories about some of these Mollie activities. One such story may have been the one recalled in 1974 by W. G. Jones of Phillipsburg, who grew up in the Wilksbarre/Scranton area. According to his tale, there was a woman who ran a "shabeen", the Irish term for a "speak-easy" or bar, near Wilkesbarre. Several Mollies reputedly came into the establishment and demanded liquor, which the woman had hidden on the premises. The woman refused to tell them where it was, whereupon they sat her down on the top of a hot stove until she changed her mind.[2]

Women were not typically the targets of the Mollies. It was men who were the usual victims of Mollie attacks, and, as noted earlier, the men were not always connected with the mines in any way. In some cases, at least, the reason for the deaths of non-mine-related individuals may have been due to mistaken identity. One typical strategy the Mollies used was to ambush a single traveler at some remote spot in the country, not unlike the highwaymen of the same and earlier periods. However, when the Mollies ambushed a lone traveler, it was to kill him. That they occasionally got the wrong man was perhaps sometimes due to misidentification arising from shade and dense foliage at the lonely spot where the ambush occurred. This would be especially true if the ambusher decided to shoot first and ask questions later. One such incident was recalled in 1989 by the grandson of the intended victim.

"In Schuylkill County you had anthracite coal being mined," began the retired minister. "And there was a mine on Good Spring Mountain. They had Irish people come in. And they had what they called, the people who lived right at the breaker and the like, they called that Irishtown. And as a little boy I remember when we'd drive over that mountain. I had a relative who worked in the lumber mill - planing mill, and we'd go up to a railroad yard to get equipment; to get cement and roofing paper.

"His lumber was all shipped in by train - by freight car. And, of course, we would go by these somewhat hovel homes, and as children we would sing a little ditty.

And it would go:

We keep the pigs in the parlor,
We keep the pigs in the parlor,
We keep the pigs in the parlor,
For we are Irish too.

"Oh, the mines were terrible. My father worked in the mines as a young boy at the breaker picking slate. He had a heart condition from rheumatic fever as a small child. He couldn't take it. My the conditions in the mine were terrible; how they had to work. So then they began to get labor trouble starting. And Mollie Maguire - the name comes from over in Ireland. So if superintendents weren't as lenient toward them as they felt they should be, they would harass them. And actually they would torture them; hold their hand to the hot plate of the stove. In fact, that was the beginning of the Pinkerton Detective Agency. They were hired to infiltrate and break up the Mollie Maguires.

"What they would do is, the local workers, miners, would never attack one of their own. They would always go, a whole bunch of them, to another community, and have all kinds of witnesses that they weren't around the night that the man was harassed. They had all these witnesses in the bar. They were in a bar. 'Oh, I wasn't there; I have this man, this man, and this man ...'. And it's true. They'd get somebody from another town to come in.

"Well, my grandfather was driving a team of horses, and he was going across the mountain; and somebody mistook him for a superintendent of the mines. And they shot at him. And he had been in

114

the Civil War; He knew enough that if he got down in between the horses the horses would take the shot rather than he. So he got down, and I guess he asked him, 'What the hell do you think you're doing ?'

"He yelled back, 'You're so and so. You're dirty so and so from the mine!'

'No', he said, 'I'm not!' He said, 'I'm Peter Starr. I have a farm.'

'Oh, I'm sorry!'

"Then he didn't shoot."

"Now this sounds like a contradiction, but somehow or other they caught this man and they took it to Pottsville, which was the county seat. And I think they had the trial, and my grandfather testified against the man - this was the one that did the shooting. And my mother said later on, after a number of years the man came by and was like a peddler, or walking the road; and Peter Starr asked him in to take supper. This was in Schuylkill County. This incident was at Goodspring Mountain. That's above Hegins, Pennsylvania, where they still shoot pigeons. "[3]

Mention of the Pinkerton Detective Agency in the preceding narrative leads to another chapter in the Mollie Maguire saga. The Mollies were probably only a small percentage of the total number of Irish miners. Not every Irish miner was a Mollie, but anyone who was also had to belong to the reputable national organization known as the AOH, Ancient Order of Hibernians. Irish origins were a requirement for membership in the AOH. Irishmen to a man, the Mollies did not enroll anyone who did not come from the Emerald Isle. Not one German, Welshman, or Englishman was invited to join the Mollie Maguires. It was for this reason that the man who finally helped bring the Mollies down was, himself, a red-headed Irishman named James McParlan.

By October of 1873, Franklin B. Gowen, president of the Philadelphia and Reading Coal and Iron Company, had finally had enough. Local and state officials hadn't been able to do anything to stop the attacks of the Mollies, and this lawless band of men was starting to hurt the coal company's business in a major way. In a final desperate move, Gowen went to the Pinkerton Detective Agency in Philadelphia. During a meeting with Allan Pinkerton himself, Gowen laid out the story of the Mollie Maguires and what they had done to the Philadelphia and Reading's business. Pinkerton thought his agency could help.

Allan Pinkerton had enough information about the Mollie organization that he knew he needed to find a man of special talents for the undercover work that had to be done. The man that was to do the job had to be especially astute and fearless, and, of course, Irish. Pinkerton finally found his man in Chicago, where he enlisted the services of James McParlan, a sandy-haired twenty-nine year old, who had been born in County Armagh, Ulster Province, Ireland. McParlan wasted no time. Changing his name to James McKenna, McParlan drifted into Schuylkill County in October, 1873. Within six months "McKenna" was able to become friends with some prominent Mollies and also become a member of the AOH. It wasn't long until the detective became a trusted officer of the county AOH. He was then a full-fledged Mollie. Once he was in this position, McParlan began to collect the evidence that would be needed to bring the Mollies to trial.

Although he wasn't able to stop the Mollies from carrying out more violence and attempting more murders while he was one of their members, McParlan was credited with preventing some killings by secretly passing warnings to the police. Such undercover efforts often put his very life in danger, but after two years McParlan's work began to bear fruit. Finally, in 1876, the kingpins of the Mollies were arrested and brought to trial, the key prosecution witness during the proceedings being James McParlan.

June 21, 1877, was once known as Black Thursday in the Pennsylvania anthracite country, because that's the day they hanged six Mollies at Pottsville, and four at Mauch Chunk. McParlan had done his work thoroughly. His testimony had resulted in convictions of some of the top Mollies in the Pennsylvania coal regions. Within a year there were more hangings, thus ending the careers of some of the more notorious Mollies. Men like Pat Hester, a "body-master" in Northumberland County, John "Yellow Jack" Donohue, and John "Black Jack" Kehoe, also known as "King of the Mollies", all died at the end of a rope.

Exactly one hundred years earlier, in 1777, the British were convinced that the leaders of the American Revolution would be defeated and brought to justice. Noting the three sevens in the year and the resemblance of the number seven to a hangman's scaffolding, they called it "the year of three gallows". No records seem to exist that indicate that 1877 was called the "year of two gallows" in the anthracite coal regions of Pennsylvania, but it could have been, given the excitement that the Mollie hangings created in Pottsville, and wherever a Mollie was hanged. Large numbers of people would gather in the early hours of the hanging day in order to get a good view of the executions. Here again there were parallels to one hundred years earlier in that floggings were still conducted at public whipping posts like the one in front of the Sunbury courthouse of Northumberland County in 1776. Crowds viewing public floggings must have been just as morbidly curious as those who came to see the Mollie hangings. In both cases there was no lack of "entertainment" for those who wanted to witness such things. The crowds viewing the executions got what they came to see. Oftentimes two men were hanged at the same time. Some of the men, dangling ten to fifteen minutes before their lives finally ebbed away, died horribly.

There is a sequel to these Mollie hangings, some of which has been told, and some of which has been the province of oral history and legend. It is a recorded fact that Franklin Gowen took his own life on Friday the thirteenth, 1889. Most people who knew him felt he did so because of his failure to prevent the bankruptcy of the coal company he had run for so long. Similarly, in Schuylkill County legend has it that some of the jurors who sent the Mollies to the gallows also committed suicide, while others died painful accidental deaths. The fate of James McParlan was not much kinder. It is said that around 1919 he contracted gangrene in the toe of one foot as a result of stumbling and falling into a rain gutter somewhere in the Midwest. Doctors were unable to save him and he probably suffered a somewhat agonizing death.

Long after the Mollies were hanged, their descendants harbored nothing but contempt for the coal companies. As time went on, however, the hard feelings softened, and by 1957, when they were interviewed for a book being written on the history of the region, even the ancestors of the Mollies' innocent victims had adopted a "forgive and forget" attitude. Among these folks were probably some who had made a point to destroy Allan Pinkerton's book entitled "The Mollie Maguires and the Detective", published in 1877. Local stories indicate that many of the Mollies' descendants in the northeastern Pennsylvania coal fields did try to destroy Pinkerton's book, and the story about James McParlan that it told. However, Jimmy McParlan was such a unique individual that his name would live on whether it was preserved on the printed page or not; memories of the great detective were still alive fifty years after his death.

"There was a fella by the name of Danny Campbell, who I knew at Pennsylvania Power and Light Company," declared the native son of the anthracite coal region. "He was born and raised up in the Conyngham Valley, in the Hazelton area, and his father was out in the Chicago area one time in the early 1900's. And he went to the Palmer House in Chicago, and he saw an old gentleman sitting in the lobby. He walked past this man. The old man looked up at him and he said, 'Be you Danny Campbell's son?'

"This guy was just flabbergasted. He said, 'Well, yes,' he said, 'how did you know that?'

"He said, 'I'm Jimmy McParlan'.

"And McParlan, of course, was the detective that was James McKenna - the alias he used when he was operating in the coal regions undercover. The guy had a phenomenal memory for names and faces. And McKenna at this time, or McParlan, was now in his, probably, early or late seventies, and was able to recognize Campbell in the brief encounter from that many years back."[4]

SITTING WITH THE DEAD

Grieving relatives of a dead person can, today, delegate the unpleasant tasks of internment, including burial and preparation of the corpse, to an undertaker. Seventy-five or more years ago undertakers were either scarce in rural areas or too expensive for most folks, and so families of the deceased had to rely upon themselves to see that their dead ones got taken care of properly. Necessary parts of this activity, which the Pennsylvania Dutch called *ausleje* [1], were washing of the body and packing the corpse in ice to preserve it. However, survivors' obligations did not stop there, or so the Dutchmen of those times thought. It was also once believed that it was absolutely necessary to have a death watch, or *di Wachnacht.* [2]

Belief in the necessity for a death watch was based on an ancient superstition. For centuries people thought that demons would carry away the soul of the departed unless a living person was there to guard the corpse until it was given a proper burial. But besides this supernatural motivation for the death watch there was also a more natural reason. Sometimes rats would be attracted to a body that had been poorly preserved, and these loathsome little creatures really made it obvious that someone had to take a turn *beim Dode Wache.* [2]

Needless to say, there would not be many folks who would look forward to their turn at a death watch, and for some people it was an unpleasant experience indeed. Imaginations of these individuals shifted into high gear, no doubt, as their turn came to go to the house where the corpse lay. In fact, it's probably fair to say that the stressful nature of this job resulted in two types of stories that became part of the folklore of the times: humorous anecdotes about jokes played upon people who were watching over corpses, and supernatural accounts about strange and unnerving things that happened during a death watch.

Details mentioned in some of the humorous narratives seem to preserve a record of what were probably attempts to reduce the level of fear associated with these macabre duties. As far as the supernatural accounts of death watches - well, as I said earlier, peoples' imaginations could become overactive. Just imagine yourself all alone by a corpse in an empty house. No sounds penetrate the stillness of the place except perhaps for the scraping sounds of a rat as it scurries across a wooden floor. There might also be the dripping sounds of water as the ice around the corpse slowly melts away, and, if the night wind were rising, there might also be strange shadows playing across the windows, dark clouds flitting across the moon, and the moaning sounds of the breezes that whip around the eaves of the old house. It could all be very spine-tingling, particularly if anyone really believed that demons might actually try to come to take away the soul of the departed.

Perhaps Peter Cole had convinced himself of such possibilities one moonlit night when he was set to take a turn at watching a corpse near a little town called Brave, which is on the Mason-Dixon Line in Greene County. Such an assignment would not have been too compatible with Cole's normal activities since he was a well-known folk singer and farrier who, like many others of his trade in that day, liked to use "music in their treatments as well as knowledge and horse sense." [3] Singer of songs like "There Was a Lady Lived in York", "Dumb, Dumb, Dumb", "Jackie Frazier", and many others [4], Cole was probably a fairly happy and upbeat person most of the time. However, on this particular night in the first or second decade of the twentieth century, Cole might have wished he knew more songs to sing while he was sitting all alone with a dead man. At least it would certainly seem that way, based on the story he would later tell about what had happened to him as he was riding up to the house. In fact it's amazing that Mr. Cole forced himself to stay there at all.

The house "had a rail fence running along the road," recalled a man who had heard the story directly from Pete Cole. "Behind that was a bunch of bushes, perhaps rose bushes - shrubs of some kind. He was just a little bit late, so he thought that maybe the other watcher might have left the house, but as he approached, he saw a man sitting on the front fence right by the road. He thought it was the person he was supposed to relieve, and as far as he could see it was the person. But he hollered out, 'Ain't you gone yet?'

"And without a word the person suddenly tumbled backwards over the fence and disappeared. Just about that time Pete's horse scared and took off. And by the time he got it back and went in, there was no sign of anything. I mean the corpse was there in perfectly decent shape, the fire was tended to - everything was in order. And so as he sat there and thought about it, he suddenly realized that the person on the fence was not the one he thought it was - was not his friend, but had had a long white beard, just like the old man who lay dead in the house.

" So he stopped his story there, but the implication was clear; that apparently the corpse had sat up in the little interval [between watchers]." [5]

Perhaps Pete Cole never liked to see an old man with a long white beard after that night of sitting with the dead, but most people in those days always thought of the beards as being "very nice and venerable looking".[5] I used to like to see them," recalled the same man who had just told me the story of Pete Cole's mysterious fence sitter. "You don't see them, except on family portraits anymore," he continued, almost as though he were trying to put old men with long white beards in a better light. "One time [in the 1930's] I was up there in western Greene County, going to the little town called Aleppo, and I passed over the top of a hill. Right at the top of the hill was a house and a garden - a paled in garden. It did have a picket fence - a huge garden usually did. And an old man with a long white beard was working in his garden.

"I stopped. I couldn't help stopping and telling him how nice the beard looked, and, boy, that pleased him something terrific. He came over and chatted with me, and every time I'd make a move, he'd lay his big eleven or twelve inch hand over my arm and say, 'Well, you ain't in any hurry are ya?' He liked to have a conversation, so I talked to him quite awhile. Then I went down to Aleppo. I guess I managed to get a lodging for the night somewhere. By the time I got down there it was dark. But in those days in that country you could knock on the door in the dark, and there would be no suspicions. Gangs of thieves had not started to operate yet." [5]

Long white beards apparently remained a popular facial adornment for old men, despite Pete Cole's experience, but Cole's story must have made it even more frightening for the faint-hearted who had heard it and were about to take a turn at a death watch. Timid souls like this, on the other hand, served as easy targets for those who loved to play jokes on these easily frightened watchers. Such pranks often involved doing something irreverent with the corpse, so they must have been done without the family's knowledge.

One such episode is said to have once occurred in the Bald Eagle Mountains of Clinton County, where men were taking twenty minute shifts watching a corpse and chasing rats away from the body. One of the men was "deathly afraid" to take his first turn, but he forced himself to go into the house anyway. When he entered the room where the corpse lay, he could not see it initially. Then he noticed the body standing in one corner of the room.[6]

Details of what the man did when he saw the corpse in the corner instead of on the table have not been preserved over the years, but the men that had stood the body in the corner must have had a good laugh. In fact, they probably had many good laughs over the years when they thought about the reaction the victim of their prank had when he entered the room and saw that the dead man had seemingly gotten up off the table and walked to a corner.

An even funnier story was once told around the little town of Hegins in Schuylkill County, where "there was this man who was a shoemaker." "He was sort of a fidgety guy; a scary guy," remembered this teller of Pennsylvania Dutch tales. "So some of the town ruffians thought they'd play a joke on him.

"They pretended that one of his friends or one of their friends had died, and they were going to have his wake. So they got the undertaker to go along with the ruse, and they dressed this man up in his Sunday clothing, and I guess they powdered his face to make him sort of white. Then they fixed him up in the coffin, and then they said about having a wake, where somebody always stays with the corpse through the night.

"They came and asked the shoemaker whether he wouldn't come in and spend an hour or so. After all, he had bought shoes from him all his life. How could you not go and give your respect to him? And he didn't want'a do it. He said he was too fidgety. He said, 'I don't want'a do it!' But they coaxed him, and he finally agreed. He said, 'Well, I'm behind in my work. I'll have to bring my work with me.'

"They said, 'Well, that'll be alright. You just have to be in the room, that's all. You bring your work with you.'

"So they had him come in, and these other gentlemen who were playing this joke, they stood behind some drapes. See, these establishments always have drapes, and they hid behind them. And the shoemaker brought his chair in, and was there [right beside the body]; he could work and just glance over every now and then at the corpse.

"So he began working, and the 'corpse' opened one eye and looked. The shoemaker couldn't believe this, you know. So he kept on working. Then the corpse opened the other eye. So, not gonna have that happen again, the shoemaker got up and turned his chair around. So right away the corpse comes over [with his hand] and grabs his shoulder.

"So he jumped up and went over and slammed down the lid of the coffin. And he had these nails with him, these hob nails, and he started to nail it down. He said, 'Dod du bist, und dod du bleiwe' (Dead you are and dead you stay)!

"The men hiding behind the drapes had to come out and pry the casket open, or the man in the casket would probably have smothered!" [7]

Similar tales were once "widely and commonly heard" [8] all over the Pennsylvania Dutch country. There are variations on the actions of the shoemaker, including one which has him hitting the "corpse" on the head with a hammer. But despite the humorous stories that can be told about death watches, there probably aren't too many of us today who would want to sit with the dead the way they used to do. Fortunately we don't have to anymore, and it's probably a good thing - the dead can now stay dead, confident that their former bodies won't be moved around just to scare someone.

THE THROWBACK

"When I was about eight or nine years old [in 1928 or 1929], I started to trap for skunks," recalled the lifelong trapper. "One morning I went to look at my traps, and I had a skunk; and there was two big white stripes down the back, you know. The more white that's on them the less money you get. I don't know how I killed the skunk anymore, but I killed it and took it home.

"That evening grandpa Frazier says, 'Well, put it in a bag and we'll take it down to Jerry Zettle.'

"So we went down to Jerry Zettle. He had his fur shop there in Spring Mills in Jake Lee's barn. We went down there, and Jerry was just ready to leave the fur shop to go to his home up in Georges Valley with his horse and buggy. Jerry had a big long beard. It come down to his belly. I had the skunk in a burlap bag, and I dumped it out and Jerry picked up the skunk and looked it over. And he stroked the skunk awhile, and he'd stroke his beard awhile.

"Finally he said to me, 'Son', he said, 'I can give you ten cents for it.'

"Of course, ten cents to me was a lot of money then." [1]

Many hunters and trappers have, at one time or another, encountered animals that were almost totally white. Not quite true albino, the coloration of these animals is still unusual enough to induce peoples' curiosity, except maybe for someone who has seen the oddity numerous times - a fur buyer like Jerry Zettle, for example. Jeremiah Zettle, born in 1865, was one of the best known trappers and fur traders in central Pennsylvania. He bought pelts in seven Pennsylvania

126

counties, where he was a familiar sight, with all his furs hanging from his horse and buggy or off his one-horse open sleigh in the wintertime. He also bought furs from all over the United States, Alaska, and from Canada. He would then sell them to New York fur buyers, many of whom would often come to his home in Spring Mills, Centre County, to pick out pelts. Jerry Zettle sometimes handled as high as ten thousand dollars worth of furs in a year - a considerable sum of money in those days.

In his lifetime of fur buying, Jerry Zettle probably saw a few albino furs, but whether or not he considered them of any value depends on whether the same coloration value system that was applied to skunks was also applied to other furs. If there was not a profit to be made from them, then Jerry Zettle would not have bought any. Likewise, if no one was buying white furs, then trappers would not have offered them for sale, and may have even considered any albino fur bearers that they trapped to be bad luck since it meant that for that particular night there had been one less trap for catching a profitable animal. Although this conclusion is speculative, it is not entirely without some foundation. There actually was one type of animal that was thought to bring bad luck to any person that killed it, and that animal was an albino deer.

One hundred and two year old Abraham Lincoln Maurer, of Julian, Centre County, noted that "the old folks" used to call albino deer "throwbacks". He didn't know why they used that term, but remembered that people used to say that you should never shoot a white deer, because if you did you'd never be able to shoot another deer of any kind. He thought that this saying was probably true because he had seen this very thing happen to a man who had killed a white deer. Maurer had once owned a farm near Julian, Centre County. During hunting season he would make extra money from hunters who would pay for room and board. One of his regular yearly boarders was George Moser from Cleveland, Ohio. Maurer remembered Moser as "a very good shot". He had sometimes accompanied him when he was hunting, and often noted that whenever Moser would shoot at a buck he could never hit it - the buck would just suddenly disappear back into the woods. Moser had once shot a white deer, and, said Maurer, "that's why he could never shoot another deer again." [2]

"It's bad luck for seven years," recalled another hunter. "My cousin shot one and, you know, he never shot any for about ten years. And he usually got his deer every year." [3]

"I can tell you a story about that, too," claimed a third hunter that I had asked about the white deer superstition. "This is back, oh my, that must've been right after we were married. After I was out of the service awhile. I'd say about '48, '49. There was me, and George L., and Mahlon D., my cousin. We were all three together in there hunting. And I seen a nice Y buck, and he was brown and white spotted. I couldn't hit him. I shot at him that day. George shot at him, and Mahlon shot at him, and neither one of us ever got him.

"They claim for seven years you won't shoot one - any other deer. I know another guy that shot one, Bob B. He got the hide tanned snow white. He showed me the hide. Well, the next year he got shot. Right through the elbow, during deer season." [4]

There are others who believe that even harsher degrees of punishment will befall the killer of a white stag, like this old-time deer hunter in Centre County:

"The last day of buck season we saw there was a white spike back there in Poe Valley," he began. "He'd'a been legal to shoot. It was about five minutes o' five. We come out, and there he was standing down along the creek.

"I said, 'Down there's one, do you want him?'

"Quent said, 'No, be Jesus,' Quent said, 'I wouldn't shoot him.'

"I said, 'I don't want him either."

"They say it's bad luck to shoot a white deer, you know. So, that was alright. Doe season come along; here some bastard caught him on the upper side road and shot him, and left him lay.

"I said, 'Now that don't make sense.

"Well, Ralph L. claimed that's how he lost his woman. He'd shot an albino deer the year before. He lost his wife right after he shot one. He said he'd never shoot another one. He's the one that told me.

"He said, 'I wouldn't care how big a rack he had. I'd never shoot him.'

"They claim they're bad luck.

"Then that John R. and them; they're from the coal region. They have a camp down along the - by the tunnel there. And one night they went out. There was an albino down in there somewhere. So they swore up and down they were gonna get him. They got pretty well slammed up one night, and went out spotlighting and shot him. And they started over the mountain to go to Livonia there somewhere, to some of their friends, to a camp, to show it to them.

"Hell, here when they were goin' down the mountain they had a wreck, and two of them were killed. John R. is the one that's still living; he was done up pretty bad.

"But he said he got out some way. I don't know how he done it, because it was a small car, two door. But some way he got out before the other guy did. And he got out, and then little Johnny got out, and little Johnny said,

'Are you hurt ?'

"And John said, 'Well, not that bad. I don't think.'

"He said, 'I got an awful bump on my head.'

"Here, hell, the damn shift had run right in his head. He only said a couple words, and fell over; and that was the end of 'im."

"They shot it down what they call High Valley. Now that's down the back road to Woodward. Down in there somewhere in the field. They shot it at night. It was spotlighted. That was in regular deer season. They were from Shamokin.

"Yeah, it was a big buck. I believe they said it was an eight point. That's why they wanted it. I said to get one that way I wouldn't want him. Illegal, and I don't want no albino." [5]

The superstition about killing an albino deer and the resulting bad luck that it brings is an old belief, and so has interesting roots - discovery of which requires a journey back into the world of strange Greek gods and ancient warriors.

The religion of ancient Greece consisted of an elaborate set of beliefs about numerous deities that controlled all things. One of these deities ,Diana, was considered goddess of the white light of morning, but she was also known as the "Lady of Wild Things, Huntsman-in-chief to the gods, lover of woods and the wild chase over the mountain". [6] All wild animals were thought to be sacred to Diana, but it was believed that she considered the deer to be most sacred of all. Greek legends stated that one particular white stag was her special favorite. Later civilizations had such faith in the old myths that they believed that some of their heroes had, at one time or another, actually encountered and captured Diana's white deer. Tales like this were once told about Julius Caesar, Alexander the Great, and other ancient warriors.

The old European tales make no mention of bad luck befalling anyone who kills an albino deer, but these episodes only tell of people "catching" such an animal, not killing it. Perhaps other, less well known, European versions of the tale mention that bad luck will be the harvest of anyone who kills a white deer. Since the white stag was once associated so closely with a goddess, it would at least seem likely that there must have been a belief at one time that it was a sacrilege for anyone to kill any albino deer. What would seem to be true, then, is that the legend of the white deer here in Pennsylvania is a descendant of an ancient Greek legend that migrated to England and Germany, and eventually to America.

Scholars say that the legend of the white deer is related to myths about the bright white light of dawn, but some hunters today steadfastly cling to the belief that it's bad luck to kill a white stag. In that sense the legend lives on, perhaps a traveler born in the ancient world which still journeys through the currents of time.

BLOODY RUN

More often than not, the story behind the origin of an older place name is lost forever in the mists of time. However, sometimes the basis for an unusual designation can, with enough time, effort, and luck, still be discovered. There are many place names in Pennsylvania that deserve just such research, but there are probably none more imaginative here than those used for some of our creeks. Among the more fascinating titles given to the streams here in Pennsylvania would have to be Jug Handle Run (Forest County), Fortuneteller Creek (Fulton County), Blue Sheriff Run (Forest County), Lost Creek (Juniata County), and Frozen Run (Columbia County). There are, of course, many other Pennsylvania streams with names that are just as imaginative, and you might think that with this kind of creativity the early settlers would not have used the same one twice. But despite the originality and diversity in nomenclature there have been instances where the same title has sometimes been used for different streams throughout the state. Among the more common ones like this are Wolf Run, Indian Run, Laurel Run, and Panther Run. Bloody Run is also a name that has been used multiple times, and among the more well-known streams with this title is the one at Gettysburg in Adams County.

This little battlefield creek that trickles past the huge pile of boulders known as Devil's Den was originally called Plum Run. However, on July second, 1863, the second day's battle of Gettysburg included heavy fighting around the hill known as Little Round Top. Maimed and dying soldiers, some wearing the blue uniform of the north and others the grey of the south, crawled to nearby Plum Run to rinse their wounds. Eventually there was so much blood washed into Plum Run that it turned red. The soldiers began calling it Bloody Run, and that has been its name ever since. As might be expected, the names of the other Bloody Runs in Pennsylvania come from incidents just like the story behind the Bloody Run at Gettysburg.

In Armstrong County, near Kittanning, there is another little stream that was once called Bloody Run due to an incident that occurred here during the Indian wars. During that sanguinary period in Pennsylvania's history, a frontier outpost known as Fort Armstrong was situated at Kittanning, and one day three scouts from the fort were scouring the nearby forest for signs of Indians. Eventually the scouting party came to the little stream called Fort Run, so named because it was so close to the settlers' fortress. Here the scouts noticed a duck acting as though it were trapped in a pool of water. The duck seemed to be held there by something, and its plight aroused the mens' curiosity.

All three frontiersmen leaned their muskets up against a tree, and then walked over to the bird to discover the cause of its strange behavior. Three Indians, using a cord fashioned from the inner bark of a linden tree, had anchored the duck in the pool, hoping it would lure some white men up to it. The Indians waited until the scouts bent over to get a closer look at the duck, and then they shot them down without so much as a warning war whoop. The mortally wounded soldiers fell into the creek, and their blood dyed the waters red. After that the creek was called Bloody Run, as a memorial to the scouts who died there.

There is also a Bloody Run that courses through Bedford County, and it too was named from an incident of pioneer days. Living on the edge of the frontier was always a risky proposition, and the early settlers of Bedford County experienced some of the worst Indian raids of that era. There are many spots in the county that were washed by pioneer blood, and among the most well known of such places is Tull's Hill, six miles west of Bedford. Here the Tull family, both parents and ten children, were all murdered by Indians in 1777. However, about ten years earlier, there was a small Bedford County stream that became even more famous as the site of a blood bath.

Around 1765, settlers living in the remote settlements along Tussey Mountain, Warrior Ridge, and Sideling Hill were driven to a state of outrage by the knowledge that the English were supplying the Indians with gifts and goods which probably included war materials. Rather than allow such supplies to be distributed to people they considered their enemies, Scotch-Irish frontiersmen, led by James Smith, took matters into their own hands. Smith organized about fifty men who dressed themselves as Indians. Their disguise included blackening of faces, the typical makeup of Indians on the warpath.

The Scotch-Irishmen positioned themselves above a narrow cut in the mountains, where they surprised a contingent of eighty pack horses that were "loaded with goods, chiefly on his Majesty's account, as presents to the Indians, and part on account of Indian traders."[1] Many of the pack horses were killed by the unerring rifles of the bushwhackers, and the victors carried off the spoils that had fallen with the animals. The blood from the dead and dying horses was also carried away - by the little stream that ran through here, and which, thereafter, was called Bloody Run in memory of this pre-Revolutionary War event.

It was from this incident that both the stream and the town of Bloody Run, now called Everett, got their names. James Smith and his "black boys", as they were prompted to call themselves because of their blackened faces, not only took some of the first steps toward the

American Revolution, but also left a record of these steps in the name of the little stream in Bedford County.

There is another Bloody Run that was also named for the blood that once dyed its waters. The history of this Tioga County creek is not well known at all, despite the fact that the tale does have some facets that makes it unique. Those who remember the story, like the man whose version follows, are becoming unique as well since they are disappearing as fast as the "No-name" Indians once did.

"The Indians that lived here were the 'No-name' Indians because they were outcasts from the Susquehannocks, and the Delawares, and the outcasts from the Senecas," explained a Potter County farmer who claimed to have some knowledge of the matter. "They were outcasts, kicked out of the tribe, and they were also outcasts from the northern tribes, the Senecas. And they moved in here and they joined up together. Just the same as they'd be outcasts today. Criminals, and stuff that they'd done that they didn't want them in the tribe no more. Their chief was called Willamacka. He was supposed to be a bastard son of Chief Logan that was educated in England through the graces of William Penn.

"The Indians were raiding the settlements down in Buffalo Valley and down around Lock Haven, around the island there, and down towards Williamsport. The governor thought that the Indians were coming from up here, which they were, but not these No-name Indians. They were evidently Senecas as far as we could judge, because they also come through this area, they also come by Sinnemahoning down. The governor sent the militia from Reading over here to get rid of them.

" Well, they come over here. They got over in here following the Highway Six path, and they found out there was an Indian village in Bloody Run. So they went up there and they massacred the whole bunch of them - women, children, everybody. And they were not the Senecas. They were just Indians that lived here. Well, the Indians which was part of the No-name tribe up here at Indian Run and Lyman Run found out about it. They just picked up and moved the hell out of here. So when the first settlers started to drift in there was a few of the No-names left here, and some of the settlers married into them, but the majority of them had left.

"As far as the record goes and as far as the old history up here at Bloody Run, they wiped out everybody. The story goes the stream ran blood red with their blood. That's why they called it Bloody Run. Now the people that was over in here where I live and at Indian Run, which is named after them, and over here on the ridge at Carter Camp, they just disappeared out of here. They must've took the Sinnemahoning trail and got out of here." [2]

As conclusive as the story of the No-name Indians at Bloody Run may seem, the end of the saga may still not be finished. The No-name Indians may yet have their revenge one day, at least in the opinion of the same old gentleman who recalled the events behind the naming of Bloody Run.

"William Penn, he come back here and he bought from a marker on the Lycoming Creek to a marker up at Corning to the 'big river in the west' in the state of Pennsylvania," continued the Potter County farmer. "The deed is recorded in the archives. Yeah, you'd better believe it, but it's going to be pretty hard for you to get a hold of it. It was for us. Yes sir, because of that deed, which they don't wanta recognize. Now the headquarters for that people is Canton, Ohio, today. Their tribal council meets once a year in Canton, Ohio. They know all about it. There's about four or five of these people that are

136

real prominent lawyers. About four or five of these people are doctors out there, that know all about this deed.

"Well, I don't know if they'll ever dispute it, but let's say if it ever got worth it they would. I know they're making a big stab at it up here at Binghamton, New York. Up there, that tribe up there's making a big stab at it and I think they're gonna win. I know the tribe up on the North Slope in Alaska won. You gotta understand what that deed says: 'the big river in the west'.

"Well, could it be the Allegheny when the Indians out in Ohio claimed oil rights under the same deed ? Says the big river in the west. Do they mean the Mississippi ? It kinda shook the world up when it was brought out, but it's in the archives, the deed, but we had a copy of it that we sent to Forest Oil. Hammond had gotten a copy of the damn thing somehow. Forest Oil - that's who my wife and I were working for when we done the title work through this area and put a leasing program together. After we had it all done then this damn thing came up and we was looking at five years' work maybe for nothing. Everybody pulled their neck in and shut up."[2]

Perhaps it could be considered poetic justice if today's descendants of the No-name tribe managed to reclaim some of the land of their ancestors. However, the No-names were certainly not the only ones subjected to misdirected slaughter by white men. There was also the massacre of the friendly Conestoga Indians by the Paxton boys at Lancaster in 1763. This appalling execution of innocent men, women and children virtually wiped out the last remaining members of the Susquehannock or Conestoga tribe. Today the Fulton Opera House sits on the site of the old jail where the massacre of the Conestogas took place. Similarly, there was another such incident in Washington County, in 1782, when another band of inflamed Scotch-Irishmen inhumanly butchered ninety-four Delaware Indians who were peaceable Moravian converts. Of the ninety-four, sixty-four were women and children.

Details of the massacre of the Conestogas in Lancaster and of the Delawares in Washington County are both recorded in the history books. However, the massacre of the Indians at Tioga County's Bloody Run does not seem to be preserved in any of that county's histories. Likewise, these same sources make no mention at all of No-name Indians, or of a chief named Willamacka. This lack of supporting documentation makes the whole legend seem that much more intriguing - a puzzle that seems as obscure as the deed which refers to the "big river in the west".

The story of Tioga County's Bloody Run is, therefore, interesting in at least two respects. First of all, the contest for the land through which the little stream courses may not yet be over. Secondly, all of the other Bloody Runs in Pennsylvania got their names by being dyed by the blood of white men. Tioga County's Bloody Run, on the other hand, appears to be the only one in the state that is named from the blood of Indians.

Footnote: Bloody Run Flows into Elk Creek, about two miles south of Watrous, Tioga County, and just opposite the ridge known as Elephant Mountain.

BEYOND BELIEF

Most of us would probably classify the following narratives as "tall" tales, or outright lies, since they are so unbelievable and contain what appears to be gross exaggeration. However, when you hear the person who actually experienced the episode talk about it in honest and sober tones, and describe things in graphic detail, then you begin to wonder what is real and what is not. Sometimes when a person sees something so strange that they doubt their own eyes, they also either doubt their sanity or conclude that what they saw was truly extraordinary. On the other hand, trying to get the rest of the world to reach the same conclusion is often humiliating and frustrating, and so many people who have experienced such things don't publicize their odd adventures.

Certainly the fear of being ridiculed or being thought of as mentally imperfect is reason enough for most people to keep their strange experiences to themselves. However, as the initial shock wears off and some self confidence returns, trusted friends and relatives may be told of the incident, as though just talking to another human being about the nightmarish event will somehow make it seem less real. Indeed there are cases where people tell of seeing things that are so bizarre, but yet so real, that their stories cause many of us to say demeaning things like "he's one brick short of a full load", "her elevator doesn't go all the way to the top", or "the light's on but nobody's home". On the other hand, the person who saw the event is certain that it was not an hallucination, not a trick of light and shadow, and not images caused by some sort of mental lapse. There is no way you can change their minds, and they stubbornly stick to their stories. However, in some cases this persistence and the durability of their tales has resulted in some interesting discoveries.

Sometimes you can say that tricks of light and shadow have caused people to see things that weren't really there, and sometimes that will be true. However, when details of strange events are so graphic and when the person who had the experience is perfectly healthy and mentally acute, then it becomes more difficult to find natural explanations behind the episode. To put this in some kind of perspective, however, we should keep in mind that in the past, people have reported seeing some very strange things that were, to the scientific community and to the public at large, totally unbelievable, but which, as time and knowledge advanced, were determined to have perfectly natural explanations.

The typical public reaction to reports of things like sea monsters huge enough to attack ships, flaming rocks that fall from the sky, and giants that rise out of the sea has been total disbelief and ridicule. However, over the years science has caught up to the observational level of the common man, and has verified the existence of the giant squid, meteorites, and temperature inversions that create some strange sights on the high seas. Medieval Norsemen were the first to claim that there were giant beings that rose up out of the sea, and the stories would be repeated time and time again, refusing to go away and even being reaffirmed as centuries passed. Science was finally able to explain the phenomenon when the stories were taken seriously and subjected to research. It was discovered that when a whale or walrus pokes its head and part of its body above the water, and the correct set of air and water temperatures exist, mirages can be observed, if seen from the correct height and angle, that greatly elongate the bodies of these sea creatures. In fact, the distortion can be so great and so complete at times that the mirage reminds observers of a giant merman who is rising out of the sea to prey upon some hapless ship.

Of course, not all tall tales like these result in the discovery of some new natural phenomenon, but they do cause us to wonder if we really know everything about the world around us. In fact, it seems reasonable to think that the tall tales that are found to have some natural basis should encourage an open-mindedness when it comes to evaluating the others like them. Readers should keep this thought in mind when they try to decide whether the following tales are fact or fancy. The story of the ghostly cow and the episode of the phantom team are separate incidents experienced by two Centre Countians in the early years of this century.

The first unusual episode occurred in Voneida Gap, a wild defile near the little village of Potters Mills, Centre County. This natural mountain passage cuts through First and Kohler Mountains and eventually intersects the road leading to Decker Valley at the place known as "The Crossroads". If the traveler continues straight through the intersection, he will eventually reach the Big Poe Mountain country and will be treated to some fantastic views of a wild and unsettled region. The gravel mountain road through Voneida Gap can be rough in places, and it is especially challenging in wet weather, but the trip is worth taking for anyone who likes to explore little-visited corners of Penns Woods. While passing through Voneida Gap, the traveler will notice some impressive rock formations along the west side of the byway, one of which is the ledge that is mentioned in the first narrative. The tale was told to me by the woman who experienced it: a quiet mountain girl of eighty-three years who recalled a fantastic adventure she experienced while going to a "camp meeting" back in the hills.

"I was goin' in Voneida Gap down here", began the little lady who was born when Teddy Roosevelt was president of the country. "[There] was three girls, and it was my cousin, who was a boy, and another guy. We were just kids really; I suppose fifteen, sixteen. There was a big meetin' in there. It was way up in. And when we went in - maybe you don't want to hear this bad word!

"We walked in. We followed the buckboard, you know. Clark Yeader and his wife Elizabeth, we just called her Lizzy, was in the buggy, in this buckboard - that's what they used to call them. We weren't up very far 'til Jay Yeader said, 'What would you do if the Devil come out here and asked you to shovel coal?' He said, 'I'd tell him to wait until I got home and got my other clothes on, and then I'd shovel his coal!' Well, we went on in to church."

After they had attended the church service, which was held in the little chapel known as "the mountain church", the same party of adults and teens came back through Voneida Gap on their way home. "Of course, it was light enough," continued the mountain lady. "They had a lantern, and we were following behind. But we come out about the same place where this was said. After the buggy passed, all at once this thing just jumped down there.

"The steam come out the nostrils, and here jumped [from a rock ledge about twenty-five feet high] a big old cow that had the biggest head I ever seen on a cow. It was dark, sort of brownish, and it had a big head for the size of its body. The rest saw it too. You couldn't hear a thing. It jumped right down there where we were, [between them and the buggy] and we screamed and hollered and run.

"Oh my sister [Marion Lingle], she fell. She had both knees tore out of her socks. And the one was down ridin' in the buckboard behind; she was sittin' in there 'til we got down. They were,

142

oh further away the distance of my kitchen here, and did we ever run to get up to 'em.

"After we got down, they stopped their horse, you know, and cut out and come up with the lantern. And they looked all around, and we couldn't find a sign of anything. We looked around, you know, where it might'a been - cow tracks. There wasn't a sign of anything. After we was home a couple days, we studied this over. That cow come out at about the same place where that bad word [the Devil] was said. That's the last we went to church too!

"Nobody [else] ever said anything if they ever saw it. My dad, Calvin Lingle, used to say they'd go in there and they could hear horses, but they never seen any. Right in this Voneida Gap here!"[1]

This next incident, which is very similar to the first one as far as its supernatural overtones, took place near the small village of Colyer, Centre County. The stream mentioned in the account is Boal Gap Run, which starts somewhere up on Sand Mountain in Mifflin County. The determined little stream flows along a gap of the same name and cuts through Sand, Triester, and First Mountains before joining Britton Run and flowing into Sinking Creek in that section of Penns Valley known locally as "The Loop". Boal Gap was once a haven for panthers and wolves in the old days, and today is surrounded by Rothrock State Forest, which contains some of the finest forest land preserved in the Commonwealth. This mini-wilderness is the home of places like Treaster Kettle, Thickhead Mountain, and Krise Valley, all of which are guaranteed to satisfy even the most fastidious seeker of solitude and natural beauty. Adding to the charm of the place are the old stories, like the one about the phantom team of horses that scared two young men out of their wits one afternoon.

What makes this story particularly interesting is the fact that the gentleman who claimed to have gone through the experience became the husband of the girl who saw the phantom cow in Voneida Gap. Perhaps their affinity toward one other was a result of a common sensitivity to things only a few people tend to experience, or perhaps they were drawn together because of common psychological traits in general. Whatever the case may be, it seems one of the traits they shared was indeed a mental ability to imagine or perceive some sort of faint images or subtle events that would, for most of us, only occur in our worst nightmares.

"I know what you want'a ask me about; the time him and Roy Royer went fishin'," declared the son of the man whose unusual story I had wanted to hear for some time. "Roy and Daddy both told me that story," he continued. "They were gonna go fishin', and Roy's grandmother told them not to go, the water was too high. She said, 'If you go, I'll know about it!'

"And there was a place up there in The Loop, going in toward Vince Treaster's somewhere, that was a pretty deep hole, like a waterfall. They were little kids, and so they went, and that's right where they went, you know. There was a big rock clear across the creek, and a hole. He said that was always their fishin' hole. Daddy said they got there and set down and put their lines in. And he said they could hear these horses runnin', just like they were out on the road. He said he could see these horses, a team of dapple greys, and this wagon comin' down the creek.

"He said they heard this rattling, and he said there went this wagon and the team of horses right down over that rock, down over that waterfall, and right into the creek, and disappeared in that fall. He

144

said it looked as real as could be, those team of horses. You could hear them runnin', he said. He said him and Roy took off and went home.

"When they got home, she said right away, 'I know where you was! You boys were up at that water hole! Didn't I tell ya?'

"She was supposed to have been able to do such stuff, you know. The old man always said 'she could do more than eat butter bread!' I couldn't tell you her name. Yeah, the old man, he often went over that story. He swore by that." [2]

Some final notes on this last story are probably in order. There used to be an old German belief that "the water spirit is supposed to dwell in the willow tree, especially in those which grow alongside a stream".[3] Perhaps this old superstition caused the boys' imaginations to work overtime on that hair-raising afternoon. The expression, "she could do more than eat butter bread" was a veiled phrase used by people who believed in witches. It meant that a person was a witch. In this case, Harry Brown, born in 1905, and Roy Royer, who was about the same age, believed that Roy's grandmother conjured up the phantom team and wagon to scare them because the boys had disobeyed her. What they really saw that day is anybody's guess.

Voneida Gap - ledge of the ghostly cow

& The creek in Boal Gap

(place where the phantom team of horses was seen)

Centre County

JACK'S NARROWS

A volume containing some stories about the Indians of Pennsylvania would not be complete without mention of Captain Jack, the "Wild Hunter of the Juniata". Also sometimes referred to as the "Black Hunter" or the "Black Rifle", this early personality was immortalized through the many tales describing his battles with the native sons of Pennsylvania. Whether or not he was a real person has often been debated, and it does seem that there is a lot of confusion surrounding this mysterious character. Such puzzlement is not surprising when it is realized that the basis for the belief in Jack's existence is rooted in a single reference in one early historical record. All other historical accounts about Captain Jack more or less paraphrase an entry that appears in the *Colonial Records*, dated August, 1750:

A friend in the interior has furnished us with the following extracts from Provincial Letters, &c. which will be found interesting. We hope he will continue them; as he kindly promises to do.

"The "Black Hunter, 'the "Black Rifle," 'the 'Wild Hunter of Juniata,' the 'Black Hunter of the Forest,' is a white man; his history is this: he entered the woods with a few enterprising companions; built his cabin, cleared a little land, and amused himself with the pleasures of fishing and hunting. He felt happy, for then he had not a care. But on an evening, when he returned from a day of sport, he found his cabin burnt, his wife and children murdered. From that moment he forsakes civilized man; hunts out caves in which he lives; protects the frontier inhabitants from the Indians; and seizes every opportunity of revenge that offers. He lives the terror of the Indians and the consolation of the Whites. On one occasion near Juniata, in the middle of a dark night, a

family were suddenly awaked from sleep by the report of a gun - they jumped from their huts and by the glimmering light from the chimney saw an Indian fall to rise no more. The open door exposed to view the ' Wild Hunter.' 'I have saved your lives,' he cried, then turned and was buried in the gloom of night.

"I could give you many a remarkable tale of the 'Black Protector.' His look is as unerring as his aim. I believe however he never shoots without good excuse." [1]

The intriguing thing about the Captain Jack of legend is that such a man probably never existed. On the other hand, the events attributed to him were most likely based on actual events. This at first may seem confusing, but historians now seem to agree that the "Black Hunter" was a composite. That is, he was a mythical character whose deeds were based on episodes from a number of other peoples' lives. Many of the stories told about the most famous Indian fighters of the state, such as Sam Brady, Tom Quick, and Peter Grove, were eventually incorporated into the legends about the "Wild Hunter". Others who may have been confused with Captain Jack were the Pattersons of Tuscarora Valley. It was said that these frontiersmen were bold and daring guardians of the valley, "whose exploits furnished much of the material for the legendary history of the fictitious 'Captain Jack', the Wild Hunter of the Juniata." [2]

What seems to have confused the issue even more is the fact that there were two real Captain Jacks whose deeds were worthy of their legendary counterpart. The first of these two men was Patrick Jack, captain of a Franklin County militia unit. Descendants of Patrick Jack claimed that it was he who offered the services of his militiamen to General Braddock prior to that British General's defeat by the Indians along Turtle Creek, Allegheny County, in 1755.

The other historical Captain Jack was Captain Matthew Jack who is remembered for his actions during the burning of Hannastown, Westermoreland County, in 1782. Known for his large gray horse and his missing hand, which he had lost in fighting the British in New Jersey during the Revolutionary War, Matthew Jack was also noted for his bravery. He was the one that single-handedly scouted the Indian raiding party at Hannastown and risked his life spreading the alarm. Not altogether successful in his attempts to warn others, he arrived at the Miller homestead after "some fifty of the Indians had rushed into the blockhouse there, capturing all but a dozen of the wedding group, who fled into the woods to hide. Both bride and groom were among those who got away safely." [3]

When the Indians saw Captain Jack approaching, they fired at him, and one bullet actually came so close that it cut one of his bridle reins. The energetic and enraged captain "gathered thirty armed settlers, hurling 'coward' into the teeth of a dozen more who refused to help." [3] Later on that evening, around midnight, Captain Jack's small force was able to slip into the fort. When the Indians saw this, they retreated to the north, taking twenty prisoners with them.

The actions of Captains Matthew and Patrick Jack were not unlike those that have been related about the legendary Captain Jack. Based on these comparisons it seems certain that the legendary Captain Jack was nothing more than a role model or, as one historian put it, a "beau ideal of the period". [4] However, this distinction seemed to escape some noted historians of the Juniata Valley, since several of them have written that Jack's Mountain of Huntingdon and Mifflin Counties was named after the legendary Captain Jack. Jack's Mountain was named after a man named Jack, but this was his first name, not his last, and his story shows how folktales and history can sometimes blend together to create legend.

Near the village of Mount Union in Huntingdon County, the Juniata River cuts its way through a narrow defile in Jack's Mountain. This cut, known as Jack's Narrows, allows the Juniata's waters to slice through the mountain until they meet the massive natural barrier known as the Black Log Mountain. Here the river turns ninety degrees in order to flow on to the Susquehanna.

The Juniata's water seems placid at times, as it flows through this peaceful cut in the mountain, but there was a time when danger, in the form of hostile Indians, lurked here. According to area legend, Jack Armstrong, a local Indian trader, found out how dangerous this place could be one day when he was traveling through these narrows and suddenly realized he was being pursued by a band of warriors. The old tale claims Armstrong was carrying a leather bag filled with gold and silver, profits of his lucrative trading business, which slowed him down considerably. Realizing he had to lighten his load if he was going to survive, the trader managed to conceal his heavy treasure somewhere among the rocks, and escaped into the fastnesses of Black Log Mountain. The old legend concludes by stating that Armstrong never returned to find his hidden cache, and that, to this day, no one has ever discovered it.

Jack Armstrong was not an Indian fighter, but he most assuredly had enemies among them, given the type of business he conducted. Indian traders, in general, were distrusted by the Indians because of the traders' dishonest ways and contemptible trafficking in whisky, rum, and other hard drinks. Considered "the vilest of our own inhabitants" [5], some traders were even convicts that had been deported from Great Britain and Ireland.

Despite their sordid reputations, the traders have to be given credit for being a fearless and hardy bunch of men. They spent many lonely days on the wilderness trails, challenging the elements and confronting the lurking dangers of uncharted forests. For their night's rest they could often count on nothing more for shelter than a hollow log. Such "sleeping places" became landmarks, and it is from John Hart's sleeping place that Harts Log Valley in Huntingdon County got its name.

Such a profession was often a solitary one, and after many long days and uncomfortable nights on the trail, the traders had very little to look forward to once they got to an Indian village - other than perhaps just one more hair-raising episode. One poor trader may have experienced just such an episode at the Indian town of Standing Stone, Huntingdon County, one day, when he was asked to be a guest of honor at a sacred feast. The exact details of this story are perhaps embellished, but the events may be somewhat representative of the predicaments a trader could get into now and then.

It seems that during the spring of 1750, the Indians around the Indian town called Standing Stone announced that there would be a "grand feast" during the first full moon of September (the city of Huntingdon, Huntingdon County, now sits on this site; however, there is still a standing stone here to memorialize the sacred totem of the Indians that once called this place their home too). One trader, who was well known to these Indians, was given a "pressing invitation" to attend the festivities, which were to be attended by six or eight different tribes.

Seeing an opportunity to make a large profit, the old entrepreneur loaded up a pack train with great quantities of rum and set out from Lancaster. He arrived a day early and found the place set up for a large gathering. The following day the exercises began with religious activities of one sort or another. The next day the ceremonies were to conclude with "a very solemn and impressive ceremony", and the Indians expressed a strong desire for the trader to be present. In what later was described as "an evil moment", he agreed to attend.

At sundown the next day, the trader noticed the warriors building a large bonfire. Later, when the flames reached their maximum height, the Indians began a feverish dance around the inferno. After the fire had burnt down considerably, the braves then brought several live dogs from out of a nearby wigwam and threw the poor animals onto the fiery bed of coals, where the canines soon expired. This was repeated until ten dogs had been half-roasted on the glowing embers.

Nauseated by the pungent smell of the roasted dogs, the trader decided to call it an evening, but the Indians insisted that he must stay until the end of this sacred ceremony. Deciding it might be best not to anger his hosts, the trader concluded he would see things through, particularly since the dead dogs would all soon be consumed in the fire. However, this assumption proved to be a serious mistake, as the trader soon noticed five or six medicine men removing the carcasses from the coals and cutting them into pieces. They then placed these "fillets" onto wooden platters and began offering pieces to each chief, who ate them with gusto.

"At last they came where I was sitting, among the only sober chiefs in the party," continues the narrative that is supposedly told from here in the trader's own words. *"The stench of the half-roasted dogs was awful. One of them came with his trencher to me, and offered me a piece, - a choice piece, too, as I was an invited guest, being a piece of the most unclean part of the entrails. 'Thank'ee,' said I; 'never dine on dog.' But this did not satisfy them. One of the prophets, laboring under the effects of about a quart of my rum, insisted on me*

eating what was offered me. I again declined, when one of the chiefs informed me that it was a very sacred feast, and unless I partook of my allotted portion I would highly insult the Indians, and some of those intoxicated might deprive me of my scalp.

"The thing was no longer a joke, and I seized the piece of dog entrail and put it in my mouth, in hopes of spitting it out; but they watched me so close that by one mighty effort I managed to swallow it. I did not wait to see the end of the feast; I had my portion and thought I might as well retire. I started in the direction of Aughwick, and every half mile the nauseous dog served every purpose of a powerful emetic. I was a much sicker man next day than if I had drank a gallon of my own rum; and, in all my dealings with the red men, I took particular care never again to be present at any dog feast!" [6]

Humorous and fictionalized as parts of the preceding story may be, the tale does reinforce the fact that a trader's life was oftentimes a dangerous one. It was one of these many "perils of the path" that finally caught up with Jack Armstrong one day in 1744 when a warrior confronted him about a horse the trader had confiscated because he felt the brave owed him some furs. The Indian caught him alone in a secluded un-named ravine, where the two men began to quarrel. Suddenly a shot rang out and a tomahawk found its mark. That night the body of Jack Armstrong lay hidden in an unmarked grave somewhere in the narrows that would be given his name.

Historians now agree that Jack's Narrows, Jack's Mountain, and Jack's Spring were all named for Jack Armstrong, the Indian trader, and not for the legendary Captain Jack. So at least the confusion about the naming of the mountain, spring, and narrows seems to be resolved, but there is one other part to the story about Jack Armstrong's demise that remains a mystery to this day. It seems that

153

Armstrong's body was never found after he had been murdered, despite intensive efforts by his brother and eight friendly Indians.

Matters stood this way for one hundred and forty-five years, and then something so remarkable happened in January of 1889 that it made the news. The event was reported in a Huntingdon County newspaper under the title "Armstrong's Resting Place":

"For about twenty-five years, it is said, a peculiar light has been seen near the top of Rocky Ridge, at Bridgeport, a short distance west of Mapleton, which made its appearance more noticeably in the month of January of each year. Those who have seen the light thought nothing of it except that it was a strange place for a light to appear, but never thought it worth while to investigate the cause. It was left for a party of three gentlemen, A. K. Skipper, Joseph Grove and Thos. M. Logan, all good and trustworthy citizens of Mapleton, to fit out an expedition in the latter part of last month to visit the spot where the light made its appearance, and inquire into the cause. The three adventurous explorers left Mapleton in the evening, and when nearing the spot they were astonished to see three lights, which had the appearance of rockets. Each one would pop up from the ground and remain for a few minutes about three feet above the surface, and then disappear in succession. These lights were on a line and seemed to point to a larger, brighter light like that from a lantern, which swayed to and fro over a crevice in the rock. The party was satisfied that it meant something, they knew not what, and as the place where the light was could be reached better in the day time and when there would be no snow and ice on the rocks, they concluded to visit the spot again, which they did a few days afterwards.

"Supposing that there might be something buried beneath the surface where the mysterious light made its appearance, they provided themselves with picks and shovels, and began to dig. After digging into

154

the ground for a depth of six feet they came upon a pile of loose stones, which covered two large flat stones that formed a lid, upon lifting which they discovered what seemed to be the remains of a human body in a hole about three feet long. The remains were decomposed to a blackened powder, and the bones when exposed to the air crumbled into dust. The explorers made a thorough examination, and are of the opinion that some one had been murdered near that place many years ago, and the body had been secreted in this secluded spot, the only thing to mark it being the singular light, which had disappeared since the discovery was made. What caused the light is as much mystery as ever. Can it be explained upon any scientific, psychological, or mythological theory ?

"It is now conceded by many that these were none other than the remains of the notorious Jack Armstrong, an individual who resided near what is known as Jack's Spring, so named after him, on Jack's Mountain, a short distance from Mount Union. He was an Indian trader, and he and his two companions, James Smith and Woodward Arnold, were murdered by a Delaware Indian named Musemeelin, in the narrows, about the middle of February, 1744, just one hundred and forty-five years ago.

"According to John Harris, the narrows took their name from Jack Armstrong. He mentions them as 'Jack Armstrong's Narrows, so called from his being there murdered.' Harris' memorandum serves, too, to locate the scene of the massacre of Armstrong and his party. He fixes it at eight miles from Aughwick and ten miles from Standing Stone (Huntingdon) which is about the spot where the body was recently found" 7

There were some locals who argued that the remains found on Rocky Ridge couldn't have been those of Jack Armstrong. "It was too far from the river," they said. Others may have thought that the lights had something to do with Captain Jack instead of Jack Armstrong since there was a similar legend at one time about the Black Hunter.

This old tale claimed that the first settlers in the area swore that every night at midnight the ghost of Captain Jack would appear on top of Jack's Mountain, just above Jack's Spring. As if trying to remember what it had been like to be flesh and blood, the spirit would take its nightly journey down to its favorite spring, stop, take a drink from the cold, pure, water, and then return back up the mountain. At least that is what the story claimed. It may have been convincing enough, however, that it lead some folks to confuse the lights on Rocky Ridge with the reputed ghost at Jack's Spring.

Though the lights on Rocky Ridge could be explained away as a natural event related to methane gas or something similar, they nonetheless must have provided a remarkable reinforcement for those who believed in one of the superstitions related to such phenomena. The belief that lights such as these often could be seen over the hidden grave of a murdered person was a common idea of those times. However, another superstition related to such lights was that they indicated spots where treasure was buried. The newspaper article about the men who uncovered the grave and found the bones did not say anything about whether or not the same men did any excavating where the three other lights were popping up out of the ground. Perhaps what really drew the men to the lights was a belief that Jack Armstrong's treasure was buried there. If treasure hunting was on their minds, the men apparently chose to keep the results of this part of their expedition a secret. If, on the other hand, they did not dig for treasure there, they may have missed an opportunity to get rich and to reinforce belief in one other old superstition.

The Standing Stone, Huntingdon County

Described by John Harris, in 1754, as being fourteen feet high and six inches square, a stone similar to this one was highly revered by the Indians of the area. Indian war parties gathered around it to celebrate their victories, and the original stone was etched with many petroglyphs. The Indians believed that ill fortune would befall their tribe if the stone were ever stolen. They removed it themselves after Pennsylvania purchased the land from the Iroquois. A replica of the stone, which stands on Penn & Third Streets, was erected by the townspeople of Huntingdon. It bears the following inscription:

Onojutta,

Juniata,

Achsinnink.

Erected September 8, 1896

As a memorial of the Ancient Standing Stone,

Removed by the Indians in 1754

157

FOOTNOTES TO THE TALES

I. The Black Ghost of Scotia
    1. Leavitt, Don, 'Iron Ghost Town',
       Published in *Town & Gown Magazine,* Jan., 1974, p. 8
    2. Brueggebors, Barbara, 'Old Killing Still Fresh in Memory',
       article published in the *Centre Daily Times of* State College, Nov., 1985
    3. Recollection of Foster W. Frazier, as remembered by his daughter,
       miss Ida Frazier.
    4. Brueggebors, Barbara, 'Murder tale hangs over The Barrens',
       Centre Daily Times, 10/31/1985
    5. Manchester, Hugh, recorded 11/6/81
    6. Linn, John Blair, *History of Centre and Clinton Counties, Pa., 44*

II. Juniata Gap
    1. Harting, James E., *Extinct British Animals,* 125
    2. Harting, *ibid.,* 181-183
    3. Harting, *ibid.,* 192
    4. Hain, H. H., *History of Perry County, Pa.,* 155-156
    5. Walker, Herbert, 'Rafting Days in Penns Valley',
       Centre County Heritage (1956-1975), 149
    6. Thornton, Frances, 'The Scotch-Irish: Pioneers of the Pioneers',
       Centre County Heritage (1956-1975), 58
    7. McKnight, W. J., *Pioneer Outline History of Northwestern Penna.,* 120
    8. McKnight , W. J., *ibid.,* 177
    9. McKnight, W. J., *ibid.,* 120
    10. Meginess, John F., *Otzinachson,* 439
    11. Maurer, Abraham Lincoln, interviewed 5/25/74
    12. Hohman, John George, *Pow-Wows, or The Long Lost Friend,* 12

III. Through the Veil
    1. Sipe, C. Hale, *The Indian Wars of Pennsylvania,* 821-23
    2. Musser, Clarence, interviewed 8/28/71
    3. Tantaquidgeon, Gladys, *Folk Medicine of the Delaware,* 104
    4. Bayard, Samuel, recorded 12/26/77
    5. Furnas, J. C., *The Americans,* 240
    6. Davis, Ken, recorded 2/11/90

IV. Snakes, Snakes, Snakes
    1. Brendle, Thomas R., and Troxell, William S.,
       'Pennsylvania German Folk Tales, Legends,

More Pennsylvania Fireside Tales

Once-upon-a-time Stories, Maxims, and Sayings',
Proceedings of the Pennsylvania German Society, Vol., L., p. 191.
2. Bumbaugh, L. W., recorded 8/22/89
3. Rung, Albert M., *Rungs Chronicles of Pennsylvania History,* 333
4. Brendle, Thomas R., and Troxell, William S., *op. cit.,* 202
5. Bayard, Samuel, recorded 12/26/77
6. Auman, Wilbur, recorded 11/19/88
7. Wagner, J. Ernest, recorded 11/19/88
8. Zettle, Roy, recorded 6/23/90
9. Brown, Harry Jr., recorded 5/5/88
10. Brendle, Thomas R., and Troxell, William S., *op cit.* 187
11. 'Rolling hoop snake story gathers color',
    newspaper article of unknown date and author which appeared
    in the *Centre Daily Times* of State College about 1990.

V. The Lower Fort
1. Montgomery, Thomas L., editor,
   Frontier Forts of Pennsylvania - Vol. I, 578
2. Linn, John Blair, *History of Centre & Clinton Counties, Pa.,* 299
3. Stover, Ray, recorded 5/19/89
4. Meyer, Dorothy, interviewed 10/25/80, 11/24/72
5. Linn, John Blair, *op. cit.,* 19
6. Linn, John Blair, *ibid.,* 20
7. Brendle, Thomas R., and Troxell, William S.,
   'Pennsylvania German Folk Tales, Legends,
   Once-upon-a-time stories, Maxims, and Sayings',
   Proceedings of the Pennsylvania German Society, Vol. L, 208
8. Sipe, C. Hale, *The Indian Wars of Pennsylvania,* 460
9. Sipe, C. Hale, *ibid.,* 830

VI. Spell-bound
1. Kuhns, Oscar,
   The German and Swiss Settlements of Colonial Pennsylvania, 86
2. Korson, George, *Pennsylvania Songs and Legends,* 5
3. Brendle, Thomas R., and Troxell, William S.,
   'Pennsylvania German Folk Tales, Legends,
   Once-upon-a-time stories, Maxims, and Sayings',
   Proceedings of the Pennsylvania German Society, Vol. L, 98-99
4. Auman, Clayton, recorded 10/31/81, and quoted from
   Gregg Township Bi-Centenial, 200 Years Remembered,
   A. M. Blunt, editor, p. 77
5. Steiger, Randall, recorded 5/4/88

4. Dyke, S. E., *The Pennsylvania Rifle*, 35
5. Hain, H. H., *History of Perry County, Pa.*, 128
6. Sipe, C. Hale, *The Indian Wars of Pennsylvania*, 645
7. Sipe, *ibid.*, 743

XII. Ridden
1. Hohman, John George, *Pow-Wows, or The Long Lost Friend*, 8
2. Hohman, *ibid.*, 48
3. Hohman, *ibid.*, 40
4. Korson, George, *Black Rock*, 153
5. Bayard, Samuel, recorded 12/26/77
6. Hardwick, Charles, *Traditions, Superstitions, & Folklore*, 233
7. Brendle, Thomas, R., and Troxell, William S.,
   'Pennsylvania German Folk Tales, Legends, Once-upon-a-time stories,
   Maxims, and Sayings',
   Proceedings of the Pennsylvania German Society, Vol. L, 147
8. Hufford, David J., *The Terror That Comes In the Night*, title.
9. Hufford, *ibid.*, 152
10. Hufford, *ibid.*, 151

XIII. Dead for Three Days
1. Boring, Paul, recorded 7/9/94
2. March, Mrs. Alverta, recorded 7/4/94

XIV. Mollie Maguire Memories
1. Sassaman, Grant M., editor,
   Pennsylvania, A Guide to the Keystone State, 76
2. Jones, W. G., interviewed 2/2/74
3. Bair, Rev. Lawrence, recorded 11/2/89
4. Eckenrode, C. W., recorded 9/18/89

XV. Sitting With the Dead
1. Korson, George, *Black Rock*, 290
2. Brendle, Thomas R., and Troxell, William S.,
   'Pennsylvania German Folk Tales, Legends,
   Once-upon-a time Stories, Maxims, and Sayings',
   Proceedings of the Pennsylvania German Society, Vol. L, p. 212
3. Bayard, Samuel P., 'The British Folk Tradition', in
   Pennsylvania Songs and Legends, George Korson, editor, p. 38
4. Bayard, *ibid.*, pp. 53, 56
5. Bayard, Samuel P., recorded 12/26/77
6. Musser, Clarence, interviewed 11/21/71

7. Bair, Rev., Lawrence E., recorded 11/2/89

XVI. The Throwback
1. Frazier, Robert, recorded 6/4/82, 2/13/88
2. Maurer, Abraham Lincoln, interviewed 5/25/74
3. Auman, Wilbur, recorded 11/19/88
4. Brown, Harry, Jr., recorded 5/5/88
5. Rowles, Ray, recorded 5/26/88
6. Hamilton, Edith, *Mythology*, 31-32

XVII. Bloody Run
1. Egle, William H., *History of the Commonwealth of Pennsylvania*, 376
2. Heggenstaller, Howard, recorded 11/16/89

XVIII. Beyond Belief
1. Brown, Gladys, recorded 4/23/88
2. Brown, Harry Jr., recorded 5/5/88 & 5/21/89
3. Stoudt, Rev. John Baer,
The Folklore of the Pennsylvania Germans, 58-59

XIX. Jacks Narrows
1. Wagner, Shirley A., 'Captain Jack - Man or Myth?'
Pennsylvania History Magazine, April, 1979, pp. 99-118
2. Hanna, Charles A., *The Wilderness Trail, Vol. II*, p. 57
3. Swetnam, George, *Pittsylvania Country*, 31
4. Sipe, C. Hale, *The Indian Wars of Pennsylvania*, 182
5. Hanna, Charles A., *op. cit.*, 307
6. Jones, Uriah J., *History of the Early Settlement of the Juniata Valley*, 27
7. Rung, Albert M., *Rung's Chronicles of Pennsylvania History*, 230

BIBLIOGRAPHY

Africa, J. Simpson,
History of Huntingdon and Blair Counties, Pennsylvania
Philadelphia, Louis Everts Co., 1883

Blunt, A. M., editor
Gregg Township Bi-Centennial, Two Hundred Years Remembered,
Gregg Township Civic Action Committee,
Spring Mills, Pa., 1977

Botkin, B. A., editor,
A Treasury of American Folklore,
New York, Crown Publishers, 1944

Brendle, Thomas R., and Troxell, William S.,
'Pennsylvania German Folk Tales, Legends,
Once-a-upon-a-time Stories, Maxims, and Sayings',
Proceedings of the Pennsylvania German Society, Vol. L,
Norristown, Pa., Pennsylvania German Society, 1944

Centre County Historical Society,
Centre County Heritage, 1956-75,
(compilation of 20 years of the society's quarterly publication
of the same name), Bellefonte, Pa., 1975

Day, Sherman,
Historical Collections of the State of Pennsylvania,
Port Washington, N. Y., Ira J. Friedman, 1843

Donehoo, George,
History of Indian Village and Place Names in Pennsylvania
Harrisburg, Pa., The Telegraph Press, 1928

Dyke, Samuel E., *The Pennsylvania Rifle*
Lancaster County Bicentennial Committee, 1974

Egle, William H., *History of the Commonwealth of Pennsylvania,*
Philadelphia, E. M. Gardner, 1883

More Pennsylvania Fireside Tales

Faris, John T., *Seeing Pennsylvania,*
  Philadelphia, J. B. Lippincott, 1919

Fisher, Sydney G., *The Making of Pennsylvania,*
  Port Washington, N. Y., Ira J. Friedman, 1896

Fletcher, Stevenson W.,
  Pennsylvania Agriculture & Country Life, 1640-1840,
  Harrisburg, Pennsylvania Historical and Museum Commission, 1971

Furnas, J. C.,
  The Americans, A Social History of the United States, 1587-1914,
  New York, G. P. Putnam's Sons, 1969

Glimm, James York, *Flatlanders and Ridgerunners,*
  Pittsburgh, University of Pittsburgh Press, 1983

Godcharles, Frederic A., *Daily Stories of Pennsylvania.*
  Chicago, Ill., Hammond Press, 1924

Grimm, Jacob, & Grimm, Wilhelm, *Grimm's Complete Fairy Tales,*
  reprinted by Book of the Month Club,
  Garden City, New York, Nelson Doubleday, Inc., 1962

Hain, H. H., *History of Perry County, Pennsylvania,*
  Harrisburg, Hain-Moore Co., 1922

Hamilton, Edith, *Mythology*
  Boston, Little, Brown, & Company, 1942

Hanna, Charles A., *The Wilderness Trail,*
  New York, AMS Press, 1911

Hardwick, Charles ,
  Traditions, Superstitions, and Folk-lore,
  (Chiefly Lancashire and theNorth of England),
  Manchester, England, A. Ireland & Co., 1872

Harting, James E., *Extinct British Animals,*
  London, Trubner & Co., 1880

More Pennsylvania Fireside Tales

Heckewelder, Rev. John,
   History, Manner, & Customs of the Indian Nations,
   Philadelphia, Lippincotts Press, 1876

Henretta, J. E., *Kane and the Upper Allegheny,*
   Philadelphia, Winston & Co., 1929

Hohman, John G.,
   Pow-wows, or The Long Lost Friend,
   (A Collection of Mysterious Arts and Remedies for Man as Well as
   Animals), originally published in the United States in the first decades
   of the nineteenth century (approximately 1820).

Hufford, David J., *The Terror That Comes in the Night,*
   An Experience-centered Study of Supernatural Assault Traditions,
   Philadelphia, University of Pennsylvania Press, 1982

Hunt, Robert, *Popular Romances of the West of England, Or The Trolls, Traditions,*
   and Superstitions of Old Cornwall, Bronx, N. Y., R. B. Blom, Inc., 1916

Jones, Uriah J., *History of the Early Settlement of the Juniata Valley,*
   Harrisburg, Telegraph Press, 1889

Klees, Frederic, *The Pennsylvania Dutch,* New York, Macmillan Co., 1971

Korson, George, *Black Rock, Mining Folklore of the Pennsylvania Dutch,*
   Baltimore, Johns Hopkins Press, 1960

Korson, George, *Pennsylvania Songs and Legends,*
   Baltimore, Johns Hopkins Press, 1960

Kuhns, Oscar, *The German and Swiss Settlements of Colonial Pennsylvania,*
   A Study of the So-called Pennsylvania Dutch,
   New York, Eaton & Mains, 1901

Linn, John Blair, *History of Centre and Clinton Counties, Pennsylvania,*
   Philadelphia, Louis H Everts Co., 1883

McKnight, William J., *Pioneer Outline History of Northwestern Pennsylvania,*
   Philadelphia, Lippincott Co., 1905

More Pennsylvania Fireside Tales

Meginess, John F., *Otzinachson, A History of the West Branch Valley,*
Williamsport, Pa., Gazette Printing House, 1889

Mitchell, J. Valentine., *It's An Old Pennsylvania Custom,*
New York, TheVanguard Press, 1947

Montgomery, Thomas L., editor, *Frontier Forts of Pennsylvania,*
Harrisburg, Pa., Pennsylvania Historical Commission, 1916

Rung, Albert, *Rungs Chronicles of Pennsylvania History,*
Huntingdon, Pa., Huntingdon County Historical Society, 1984

Sassaman, Grant N., editor, *Pennsylvania, A Guide to the Keystone State,*
Pennsylvania Writers Project,
New York, Oxford University Press, 1940

Sipe, C. Hale, *The Indian Chiefs of Pennsylvania,*
Butler, Pa., Ziegler Printing Co., 1927

Sipe, C. Hale, *The Indian Wars of Pennsylvania,*
Harrisburg, Pa., The Telegraph Press, 1931

Stoudt, Rev. John Baer, *The Folklore of the Pennsylvania Germans,*
The Pennsylvania German Society, Lancaster, Pa.,
The New Era Printing Co., 1916

Swetnam, George, *Pittsylvania Country,*
New York, Duell, Sloan & Pearce, Inc., 1951

Tantaquidgeon, Gladys, *Folk Medicine of the Delaware,*
Harrisburg, Pa., Pennsylvania Historical Commission, 1972

Tome, Phillip, *Pioneer Life, or Thirty Years a Hunter,*
Baltimore, Md., Gateway Press, 1989, reprint of the 1854 edition.

Wagner, Shirley A., 'Captain Jack - Man or Myth?',
Pennsylvania History Magazine, Vol. XLVI, No. 1,
April, 1979, pp. 99-118

Wallace, Paul W., *Indians In Pennsylvania,*
Harrisburg, Pennsylvania Historical Commission, 1970

Jeffrey R. Frazier

This is a second (hardcover) edition of Volume II in the series entitled *Pennsylvania Fireside Tales*. Other volumes that have been published in the series include *Pennsylvania Fireside Tales, Volume I* (published in 1996) and *Pennsylvania Fireside Tales, Volume III* (published in 1999). All three volumes can be ordered directly from the author @ $12.00 per volume plus $2.00 shipping and handling costs, or they can be purchased for the same price at major bookstores, including Barnes & Noble and Borders Bookshops.